GW01607862

PROMISES FROM THE HOLY BIBLE

'He has given us his very great and precious promises'.

2 Peter 1:4

Creative Publishing
'Visual books for a visual age'

Creative Publishing
'Visual books for a visual age'

6 Pembroke Road, Moor Park, Northwood, Middlesex, England.

ISBN 0907781 24 1

First printed in 1983.

Photographs by Alan Bedding, Andrew Frank, Robert F. Hicks, Peter Hyde, John Lloyd, Paul Marsh, Adrian Neilson, David Parker, Craig Stuart-Paul, Will Shadwell.
Designed by Rodney Shepherd and Robert F. Hicks.
Typeset by Nuprint Services Ltd, Harpenden, Herts.

Coedition arranged with the help of Angus Hudson Ltd, London and printed in England by Purnell (Book Production) Ltd, Paulton, Somerset.

Introduction

The Christian faith is *positive* – it offers a Saviour, a future . . . and great promises. What are they?

Carefully explained and illustrated in this book are what the Bible says about God's promises – promises of love, joy, peace, hope, life, forgiveness, comfort and confidence.

Each chapter offers its own unique contribution. Each chapter celebrates some of the triumphs and treasures of our faith. Each chapter can be made the subject of prayer and thought and study. For the reader, here is a companion to keep at your side for encouragement and inspiration. God has much more to give us than we can ever imagine. For the study group, here is an excellent source-book and commentary. Together you will more readily discover the relevance and truth of God's Word.

At the close of each chapter you will find a prayer relating to its subject. I hope the prayer will help you to express just what you feel about God's wonderful promises.

Michael Perry

Promises from the Holy Bible

For many people the enjoyment of God's Word seems at best a remote possibility. The Bible to them looks a big book, and feels an old book, especially those available in black covers. Even those editions with colour sections depicting Bible background, present a problem; they look as if they belong to a different culture from the past and somewhere 'over there'.

To many church-going people, motivation to read the Holy Bible is also a problem. The temptation to listen to sermons and allow them to become the substitute for personal reading of God's Word, is an all too frequent experience.

In producing *Promises from the Holy Bible* we hope to have provided a 'bridge' that will enable many to discover the beauty, truth, hope and lasting encouragement which many have enjoyed from personal reading of God's Word.

A great deal of thought has gone into the visual presentation in order give the maximum help, not only in reading and enjoying, but also in responding to God's living Word.

Promises from the Holy Bible can be used as a daily reading, either morning or evening.

Promises from the Holy Bible can also be read in sessions. By looking at the contents pages you will see that the sections give progressive readings. By reading a complete section at a time important truths of the Bible will become clear.

Promises from the Holy Bible is produced as a pocket book which has the benefit of being able to be slipped into a pocket or handbag quite easily.

Whether reading complete sections at a time, or being used as a daily reading aid, the following may be of help:

Read Expectantly. This is God's Word, so be prepared to receive new insights in his truth for you.

Read Deliberately. Time spent reflecting on what you've read will not be wasted. Meditation has always been a great strength in the development of Christian character.

Read Responsively. Besides the promises and blessings you can expect from the Holy Bible, there will also be challenges and new opportunities presented to you. By responding to God's Word your own life will be enriched.

Read Thankfully. The Holy Bible is not meant to conceal God but reveal him. As you discover more about him, his Son, the Holy Spirit, the way of salvation and the Christian life, be thankful; enjoy everything he has in store for you.

It is the prayer of many who have been involved in bringing this book to you that through it you will discover that the Holy Bible is God's Word – a book not to be afraid of, but *enjoyed.*

The text in this edition has been benefited by the helpful notes and prayers of my friend Michael Perry.

Robert F. Hicks

General Content

Book 1: The Promise of Love

God's love is a family love – the love of a caring father for a wayward child. His is a love that knows no limit; in Jesus he showed how very far his love would go to meet our desperate need. In Jesus, too, we can share in the dimensions of that love; filled with his Spirit we can bring others into God's loving family.

Book 2: The Promise of Joy

Many people are deceived into thinking that religion is dreary – the Christian faith certainly isn't; it can be filled with excitement and joy! Not a frivolous passing joy that leaves you unsatisfied, but a deep, lasting joy that has its roots in God's promise and presence; a joy that no depth of sorrow can really extinguish.

Book 3: The Promise of Peace

Peace is a word over used by anyone who has a political axe to grind. Set that aside when you think about the peace of God. His peace is given through Jesus to the person with a humble heart. It is the peace that comes to us when we know our wrong-doing is forgiven and our future is in God's hands. It is the peace we must share if we are to be true to our Christian calling as 'peace-makers'.

Book 4: The Promise of Hope

'Hope springs eternal' – they say. But the only source of eternal hope is the resurrection of Jesus Christ. God raised him from the dead – for us. By this we know that our future is assured; for in Christ we too may have life out of death. And the Christian hope affects not just the eternal future, but the here-and-now.

Book 5: The Promise of Life
All life is God's creation; in him 'we live and move and have our being'. The Bible tells us that we can be physically alive and well, but spiritually like a skeleton! It is Jesus, who said 'I am life', who adds the vital ingredient. In him we may share the experience of the early Christians – they opened their hearts to the life-giving Spirit of Jesus.

Book 6: The Promise of Forgiveness
Do we need it? – forgiveness? Unless we are perfect, yes we do! At supper on the night before he died, Jesus took a cup of wine and said to his closest followers, 'This is God's new agreement with you – sealed in my blood – for the forgiveness of sins.' We must see things the way Jesus did, then we shall know ourselves as we truly are, and be able to receive God's promise of forgiveness. What a new freedom this could give to our lives and hopes!

Book 7: The Promise of Comfort
The God of the Christian faith is like no other! He does not sit somewhere in security while we cry and feel pain, while we are anxious and we mourn. No, in Jesus Christ he came into our world, not merely to 'sympathise', but to share the very worst that can ever happen to any one of us. So the comfort God gives is borne of his bitter experience. And because he is God – and all-powerful – it really means he can help, bringing us genuine comfort.

Book 8: The Promise of Confidence
The world is full of shattered people – who thought they had good reason to trust in money, or political power, or acts of deceit or theft, or luck, or even relatives and friends. Then they were let down! God alone never fails. A relationship with him through Jesus Christ will give us our surest confidence. Come into that relationship by offering Jesus your love, your loyalty and your life's service!

The Promise of LOVE

Book 1

The Promise of
JOY

Book 2

The Promise of PEACE

Book 3

The promise of Peace
Peace for our lives
Peace from Christ
God's peace

Peace from God
The peace we need
Jesus, the bringer of peace

Peace that unites
Peace that puts things right with God
The price of peace

Peace that dispels fear
Peace in our consciences
The war is over

Peace past understanding
Peace in our hearts
Throughout the day

Peace for difficult times
Peace in the storm
The peace of his presence

Peace for God's people
Peace for the righteous
The way of peace

Peace that reaches out
Peace for the peacemakers
'Blessed are the peacemakers'

Peace that's active
Peace in our world
Preserving the peace

Peace that's effective
Peace in our nation
God knows best

A prayer of Peace

The Promise of HOPE

Book 4

The Promise of LIFE

Book 5

The promise of Life
Life's beginnings
The giver of life

Life with a purpose
Life's realities
A life that is conscious of God

Life that comes from God
Life's new birth
Spiritual life

Life that overflows
Life's new power
The Lord of life

Life that's immortal
Life's new hope
Life out of death!

Life that's full and free
Life's greatest adventure
Life here and hereafter

Life that's confident
Life's assured future
Being sure of life

Life that's strong
Life's source of strength
Cling to life

Life that's fruitful
Life's choices
Plan for a useful life

Life that's satisfying
Life's full stature
Feed your life, use your life

A prayer for Life

The Promise of Forgiveness

Book 6

The Promise of Comfort

Book 7

The Promise of Confidence

Book 8

Finally, brothers, whatever is true, whatever is noble, whatever is right, whatever is pure, whatever is lovely, whatever is admirable – if anything is excellent or praiseworthy – think about such things. Whatever you have learned or received or heard from me, or seen in me – *put it into practice.* And the God of peace will be with you.

Philippians 4:8–9

Promises from the Holy Bible is a combined edition comprised of the following eight books:

Book 1: The Promise of Love
Book 2: The Promise of Joy
Book 3: The Promise of Peace
Book 4: The Promise of Hope
Book 5: The Promise of Life
Book 6: The Promise of Forgiveness
Book 7: The Promise of Comfort
Book 8: The Promise of Confidence

The Promise of LOVE

The promise of love

Love's initiative

When Israel was a child, I loved him, and out of Egypt I called my son. But the more I called Israel the further they went from me. They sacrificed to the Baals and they burned incense to images.

It was I who taught Ephraim to walk taking them by the arms: but they did not realise it was I who healed them. I led them with cords of human kindness, with ties of love; I lifted the yoke from their neck and bent down to feed them.

How can I give you up, Ephraim? How can I hand you over Israel? How can I treat you like Admah? How can I make you like Zeboim? My heart is changed within me: all my compassion is aroused.

The love of a father

This beautiful passage describes God's love for his people. Despite the depth of his concern for them they ignore him, and refuse to respond to him. Like a loving father he has brought them up with tenderness and care. His life is linked with theirs and the deepest affection binds them together. Whatever they do he will not, and cannot, abandon them. To do so would be to break his own heart. This is the kind of love we can expect from God when we allow him to take us into his own family. Through Jesus Christ, we too become his people and his children. Then, St Paul says, he loves us with the love he has for his Son.

Hosea 11:1–4,8

'The deepest affection binds them together.'

Love that excels

Love's definition

This is how God showed his love among us: He sent his one and only Son into the world that we might live through him. This is love: not that we loved God, but that he loved us and sent his Son as an atoning sacrifice for our sins.

One of the teachers of the law came and heard them debating. Noticing that Jesus had given them a good answer, he asked him, 'Of all the commandments, which is the most important?' 'The most important one,' answered Jesus, 'is this: "Hear, O Israel, the Lord our God, the Lord is one. Love the Lord your God with all you heart and with all your soul and with all your mind and with all your strength." The second is this: "Love your neighbour as yourself." There is no commandment greater than these.'

God's love is unique

Despite the picture of fatherly love, we must be careful not to think of God's love only in terms of ours. We may attempt a feeble love of God, but love is truly defined by God's supreme gift of Jesus, through pain and sacrifice to be our Saviour and our Lord. Love is the source of our Christian life and also its rule. Love is the attitude of heart and mind that God commands. It's no use our protesting that we live by the rules if we do not love according to God's commandment. Love, then, is the complete gift of our heart, mind and strength – to God and to each other.

1 John 4:9,10 Mark 12:28–31

Love is the attitude of heart and mind

Love that endures

Love's quality

Love never fails. But where there are prophecies, they will cease; where there are tongues, they will be stilled; where there is knowledge, it will pass away. For we know in part and we prophesy in part, but when perfection comes, the imperfect disappears. When I was a child, I talked like a child, I thought like a child, I reasoned like a child. When I became a man, I put childish ways behind me. Now we see but a poor reflection; then we shall see face to face. Now I know in part; then I shall know fully, even as I am fully known. And now these three remain: faith, hope and love. But the greatest of these is love.

Love goes on for ever

This passage from St Paul's letter to the Corinthians has a literary beauty all of its own. It is a lesson to us to look at things with the perspective of eternity. We must realise that our petty interests are as nothing compared with the ultimate purpose of our faith – to reflect in our lives that perfect love of God.

Love has an enduring quality that surpasses everything else. Earlier in his letter to the Corinthians, Paul lists God's other gifts to the Church. Most of these are temporary and for our present situation. They are gifts for the human world, that will be outmoded in the maturity of heaven. We shall not need the props to our understanding then, because we shall know God as fully as he knows us now. Our faith and our hope will be rewarded by seeing him as he really is – pure love.

1 Corinthians 13:8–11

'Now I know in part; then I shall know fully.'

Love that is close

Love's presence

Jesus said, 'He who loves me will be loved by my Father and I too will love him and show myself to him.' 'If anyone loves me, he will obey my teaching. My Father will love him, and we will come to him and make our home with him.'

And so we know and rely on the love God has for us. God is love. Whoever lives in love lives in God, and God in him. Love is made complete among us so that we will have confidence on the day of judgement, because in this world we are like him. There is no fear in love. But perfect love drives out fear, because fear has to do with punishment. The man who fears is not made perfect in love. We love because he first loved us.

The gift of love

Our dedication to Jesus Christ is rewarded by the gift of God's love and a vision of his purpose for us. We experience this love in our lives because God 'comes to live with us'. The result is a new confidence and a freedom from fear. The experience may be immediate, or it may be gradual as God's Spirit works its way into all our thought and action. Note how John writes of love and judgement in the same sentence. God's love is not the careless indulgence that with us often passes for love. His is a moral and sacrificial love. It's not because God has let us off that we need not fear the 'day of judgement', but because – in Jesus – God loved us enough to die for us.

John 14:21, 23 1 John 4:16–19

'We love because God first loved us.'

Love all-embracing

Love's dimensions

Lord, you are all round me on every side; you protect me with your power. Such knowledge is too wonderful for me, too lofty for me to attain. Where can I go from your Spirit? Where can I flee from your presence? If I go up to the heavens, you are there; if I make my bed in the depths, you are there. If I rise on the wings of the dawn, if I settle on the far side of the sea, even there your hand will guide me, your right hand will hold me fast.

I, Paul, kneel before the Father, from whom the whole family in heaven and in earth derives its name. I pray that Christ may dwell in your hearts through faith, that you, being rooted and established in love, may have power, together with all the saints, to grasp how wide and long and high and deep is the love of Christ, and to know this love that surpasses knowledge – that you may be filled to the measure of all the fulness of God.

Praying for love

Paul prays for believing people that they may experience this indwelling of Christ in their hearts as they place their confidence in him. The tender plant of our Christian lives will begin to grow when we put down our roots into the soil of that love which is Christ himself. And however far we probe we shall never come to the end of it. Neither our minds nor our emotions can grasp its full extent. See how Paul mixes up his pictures of love – homes, roots, distances – in his intense desire to express the wonder of it. God is able to do immeasurably more than all we ask or imagine, he says.

Psalm 139:5–10 Ephesians 3:14, 15, 17–19

Lord, you protect me with your power.

*Love always protects,
always trusts, always
hopes, always perseveres.*

Love for passing on

Love's duty

Dear friends, since God so loved us, we also ought to love one another. No one has ever seen God; but if we love each other, God lives in us and his love is made complete in us.

A new commandment I give you: Love one another. As I have loved you, so you must love one another. All men will know that you are my disciples if you love one another.

If anyone has material possessions and sees his brother in need but has no pity on him, how can the love of God be in him? Dear children, let us not love with words or tongue but with actions and in truth.

Passing it on

Receiving the love of God places a happy obligation on us. Life becomes full of meaning and purposes for us as we realise that we are here to pass on God's love. If we do not pass it on, others will not see God's love in us, and will quite reasonably doubt that we know God at all. So, God's love may sound theoretical but it has a very practical outworking. Mere *words* about love are not enough. The Christian practice of love, then, involves our money and all our possessions. If God has blessed us with these, it is so that we might be better followers of Jesus Christ. Jesus invariably helped those who asked him. He helped people very often in the face of fierce opposition – sometimes by his own friends.

1 John 4:11, 12 John 13:34, 35 1 John 3:17, 18

'If anyone sees his brother in need but has no pity on him, how can the love of God be in him?'

Love for one another

Love's family

Everyone who believes that Jesus is the Christ is born of God, and everyone who loves the father loves his child as well. This is how we know that we love the children of God: by loving God and carrying out his commands. This is love for God: to obey his commands.

Jesus said, 'As the Father has loved me, so have I loved you. Now remain in my love. If you obey my commands you will remain in my love, just as I have obeyed my Father's commands and remain in his love. I have told you this so that my joy may be in you and that your joy may be complete.'

Praise be to the God and Father of our Lord Jesus Christ, who has blessed us in the heavenly realms with every spiritual blessing in Christ. In love he predestined us to be adopted as his sons through Jesus Christ, in accordance with his pleasure and will – to the praise of his glorious grace, which he has freely given us in the One he loves.

God joins us together

The fellowship of true Christian believers is wonderful and joyful. They can be conscious of being in a universal family – the family of God's love. It is a family relationship of willing obedience and happy service, an exciting and purposeful relationship. Love among Christian people is both a gift and a command. It is not an option; we cannot refuse or choose. We must all love – and that includes the active expression of our caring concern – for all our Christian brothers and sisters of whatever opinion, nationality or race.

1 John 5:1–3 John 15:9–11 Ephesians 1:3, 5, 6

Christians: the family of God's love.

Love that is for now

Love's fellowship

If you have any encouragement from being united with Christ, if any comfort from his love, if any fellowship with the Spirit, if any tenderness and compassion, then make my joy complete by being like-minded, having the same love, being one in spirit and purpose.

Dear friends, let us love one another, for love comes from God. Everyone who loves has been born of God and knows God. Whoever does not love does not know God because God is love.

Just as you excel in everything – in faith, in speech, in knowledge, in complete earnestness and in your love for us – see that you also excel in this grace of giving. I am not commanding you, but I want to test the sincerity of your love by comparing it with the earnestness of others. For you know the grace of our Lord Jesus Christ, that although he was rich, yet for your sakes he became poor, so that you through his poverty might become rich.

Love in the church

The expression of love in the church requires some effort on the part of its members. Born into us is a natural inclination to be unloving and selfish. We learn to be outward-looking and generous as we imitate the selflessness of Christ. We grow in grace and Christian maturity as we learn to give way to one another. In church we must put our insistence on right speaking and behaviour second to the Christian requirement of mercy and tenderness towards those who are not so strong in their faith.

Philippians 2:1, 2 1 John 4:7, 8 2 Corinthians 8:7–9

'Love one another, for love comes from God.'

Love that is beautiful

Love's humility

Love is patient, love is kind. It does not envy, it does not boast, it is not proud. It is not rude, it is not self-seeking, it is not easily angered, it keeps no record of wrongs. Love does not delight in evil but rejoices with the truth. It always protects, always trusts, always hopes, always perseveres.

As a prisoner for the Lord, then, I urge you to live a life worthy of the calling you have received. Be completely humble and gentle; be patient, bearing with one another in love. Make every effort to keep the unity of the Spirit through the bond of peace.

What love is not

Paul states very clearly the things that true love does not do. Boasting and pride are out, rudeness, irritability, vindictiveness, unworthy interest, hurtfulness, impatience – all these things are out for the Christian. Love is caring, trusting, open-minded, persistent, peace-making.

See how divisive are the failings listed here, and how uniting are the virtues. For too many of us, love stops short at 'bearing with' other people and gives way to all these vices. The result is disunity amongst us, and God is grieved. Our anger cannot achieve the peace that God wants. But our love can, if it is self-effacing and Christ-exalting love, where God's glory and his will matter more than our selfish desire to be vindicated. Let love prevail – not me!

1 Corinthians 13:4–7 Ephesians 4:1–3

True love produces beautiful lives.

Love that is for ever

Love's permanence

But God demonstrates his own love for us in this: While we were still sinners Christ died for us. If, when we were God's enemies, we were reconciled to him through the death of his Son, how much more, having been reconciled, shall we be saved through his life!

Who shall separate us from the love of Christ? Shall trouble or hardship or persecution or famine or nakedness or danger or sword . . . I am convinced that neither death nor life, neither angels nor demons, neither the present nor the future, nor any powers, neither height nor depth, nor anything else in all creation will be able to separate us from the love of God that is in Christ Jesus our Lord.

God's love is stronger than anything else

God has proved how much he loves us by sending his only Son, Jesus Christ, to die for us. How unattractive we must have seemed — rebels against God and stupidly lost in our own failings. If these things couldn't keep God's love away from us, what can?

Paul lists all the possibilities. But the obvious dangers of life will not prevent God's love from reaching us, nor will the hidden dangers – the unknown and unmeasured powers of darkness – they too are unable to cut us off from God's love. God's love is as powerful as Jesus' resurrected life: it overcomes death itself in order to keep us for ever close to God.

Romans 5:8, 10   Romans 8:35, 38–39

'Not anything in all creation will be able to separate us from the love of God that is in Christ Jesus our Lord.'

A prayer of love

O Lord Jesus Christ,
who loved us more than life,
come to our hearts with your burning
fire of love;
take away our coldness and selfishness
and let the loveliness of your spirit
be seen in us:
so may we grow up into you
until all our ways are love,
and love is our every word;
so may we become one in love with you
and nothing shall separate us.
Amen.

Michael Perry

The Promise of JOY

The promise of joy
- *Joy comes to Jesus' disciples*
- *The joy of resurrection*

Joy that transforms
- *Joy comes to a family*
- *The joy of discovery*

Joy for God's people
- *Joy through being right with God*
- *Joy because of what God can do for us*

Joy in God's presence
- *Joy through the Bible and Prayer*
- *The joy of God's companionship*

Joy in difficult times
- *Joy despite sorrow*
- *The joy that breaks through tears*

Joy that works
- *Joy in all circumstances*
- *The joy of living by faith*

Joy that overflows
- *Joy in the church*
- *The joy of praising God*

Joy past comprehension
- *Joy in living service*
- *The joy of being part of God's plan*

Joy that needs expression
- *Joy for the world*
- *The joy which must be shared*

Joy that lasts and lasts
- *Joy in heaven*
- *The joy of eternity*

A prayer of joy

The promise of joy

Joy comes to Jesus' disciples

Now is your time of grief, but I will see you again and you will rejoice, and no one will take away your joy.

Jesus himself stood among them and said to them, 'Peace be with you.' They were startled and frightened, thinking they saw a ghost. He showed them his hands and feet. And while they still did not believe it because of joy and amazement, he asked them, 'Do you have anything here to eat?' They gave him a piece of broiled fish, and he took it and ate it in their presence. He said to them, 'This is what I told you while I was still with you: everything must be fulfilled that is written about me in the law of Moses, the Prophets and the Psalms.'

The joy of resurrection

As Jesus promised, the disciples came through their time of grief and sorrow and found him alive again from the dead. They rejoiced to see the friend and Master they thought they had lost.

Jesus is alive today! And though he does not appear to us in physical form, yet we can be sure of his presence just the same. He finds us in our work and in our sorrows, bringing to us joy and amazement. If only the disciples had paid attention to the Scriptures they might not have become so despondent. The same is true of us; we need the constant encouragement of the word of God.

John 16:22 Luke 24:36, 37, 40–41

Springtime, the joy of new life.

Joy that transforms

Joy comes to a family

The jailer called for lights, rushed in and fell trembling before Paul and Silas. He then brought them out and asked, 'Men, what must I do to be saved?' They replied, 'Believe in the Lord Jesus, and you will be saved – you and your household.' Then they spoke the word of the Lord to him and to all the others in his house. At that hour of the night the jailer took them and washed their wounds; then immediately he and all his family were baptised. The jailer brought them into his house and set a meal before them, and the whole family was filled with joy, because they had come to believe in God.

The joy of discovery

It must be admitted that the jailer's first discovery was not at all joyful! He was responsible with his life for those prisoners, who had been freed by an earth-tremor. But Paul and Silas stayed to talk to him about the Lord Jesus: if he would only believe and trust in Jesus, he and his household would be saved. Jesus came to save us from the consequences of our sin. As the prophet Isaiah put it, 'Our punishment was upon him'. Evidently the jailer's whole family – thrilled at the good news – entered into the Christian family by the symbol of Baptism. Joy comes to families when they believe in God.

Acts 16:29–34

Joy for God's people

Joy through being right with God

Restore to me the joy of your salvation and grant me a willing spirit, to sustain me. Save me from bloodguiltiness, O God, the God who saves me, and my tongue will sing of your righteousness. O Lord, open my lips, and my mouth will declare your praise.

Praise the Lord, O my soul; all my inmost being, praise his holy name. Praise the Lord, O my soul, and forget not all his benefits. He forgives all my sins and heals all my diseases; he redeems my life from the pit and crowns me with love and compassion. He satisfies my desires with good things, so that my youth is renewed like the eagle's.

Joy because of what God can do for us

Some of these Psalms were written as ready prayers to meet the needs of worshippers who wanted to express their feelings towards God. Sometimes their feelings, like ours, were of an oppressive guiltiness. Everything was black and hopeless – a shuttered room where the joy of God could not enter. The writers of the Psalms were realistic and down-to-earth; they knew that people needed to be told of the forgiveness that God could bring. God gives us the joy of a clear conscience when we tell him how sorry we are for the things we have done wrong.

Psalm 51:12, 14–15 Psalm 103:1–5

The Simplon Pass, Switzerland.
'Your youth shall be renewed like the eagle's'.

Joy in God's presence

Joy through the Bible and Prayer

Praise be to you, O Lord; teach me your decrees. With my lips I recount all the laws that come from your mouth, I rejoice in following your statutes as one rejoices in great riches. I meditate on your precepts and consider your ways. I delight in your decrees; I will not neglect your word. Do good to your servant, and I will live; I will obey your word. Open my eyes that I may see wonderful things in your law.

I tell you the truth, my Father will give you whatever you ask in my name. Until now you have not asked for anything in my name. Ask and you will receive, and your joy will be complete.

The joy of God's companionship

As we get to know God, we delight in discovering more about him. The Bible's rules for living may have seemed dreary at one time. Now they begin to excite our interest. Soon we shall find them a greater joy than any human wealth. As our relationship with God becomes stronger, we shall grow more confident in our praying. God always honours whatever we say to him – he loves to hear us speaking. So we should be relaxed whenever we approach him, and pray from our heart. We will pray in the confidence that he answers prayer. When he does answer, our joy will know no bounds.

Psalm 119:12–18 John 16:23, 24

As our relationship with God becomes stronger, we shall grow more confident.

Joy in difficult times

Joy despite sorrow

Dear friends, do not be surprised at the painful trial you are suffering, as though something strange were happening to you. But rejoice that you participate in the sufferings of Christ, so that you may be overjoyed when his glory is revealed.

Blessed are those who are persecuted because of righteousness, for theirs is the kingdom of heaven. Blessed are you when people insult you, persecute you and falsely say all kinds of evil against you because of me. Rejoice and be glad, because great is your reward in heaven.

The joy that breaks through tears

Let's be realistic! Life is not all happiness. Times of sorrow and pain come to everyone. Christians are not exempt from these problems; it would be wrong if they were. We are in this world to care and to understand and to sympathise. We cannot do it if we have not experienced the same sufferings as other people. In this way we follow our Lord Jesus Christ, who chose to accept the worst kind of suffering in order that he might know and share our deepest needs. The Bible warns us that there will be times of persecution and hardship. But, for the believers, there will be joy through tears.

1 Peter 4:12–13   Matthew 5:10–12

Suffering is a mystery, but it can produce beautiful lives.

Shared happiness.

Joy that works

Joy in all circumstances

Those who sow in tears will reap with songs of joy. He who goes out weeping, carrying seed to sow, will return with songs of joy, carrying sheaves with him.

Be joyful always; pray continually; give thanks in all circumstances, for this is God's will for you in Christ Jesus.

Paul wrote: 'I have learned to be content whatever the circumstances. I know what it is to be in need, and I know what it is to have plenty. I have learned the secret of being content in any and every situation, whether well fed or hungry, whether living in plenty or in want. I can do everything through him who gives me strength.'

The joy of living by faith

Learning to trust God completely – for everything – takes time and spiritual experience. Paul, the great adventurer, a man with so much intelligence and so many gifts, learned in the school of Christian living that God was trustworthy.

It is as we practise prayer, and develop in ourselves a spirit of thankfulness, that we really discover God's help is sufficient.

Psalm 126:5, 6 1 Thessalonians 5:16–18 Philippians 4:11–13

Joy is the harvest of trusting God.

Joy that overflows

Joy in the church

Speak to one another with psalms, hymns and spiritual songs. Sing and make music in your heart to the Lord.

Praise the Lord. Praise God in his sanctuary; Praise him for his acts of power; praise him for his surpassing greatness. Praise him with the sounding of the trumpet, praise him with the harp and lyre, praise him with tambourine and dancing, praise him with the strings and flute, praise him with the clash of cymbals, praise him with resounding cymbals. Let everything that has breath praise the Lord. Praise the Lord!

The joy of praising God

Gloomy churches and gloomy church-people are a contradiction of the good news of our salvation in Christ. Even the tone-deaf can express joy in harmony of love, forgiveness and welcome. But for all the gift of music, there is an obligation to match our praise to the high call of worshipping God. No perfectionism, clucking tongues or raised eyebrows should prevent the worthy expression of our love for God in any truly musical way. From tambourine to flute, from trumpet to cymbals, we tell the wonders of God in word and movement. We pause only to make sure that our worship is truly based in the Spirit and in the Scripture. Bring praise to the Lord!

Ephesians 5:19 Psalm 150; 1–6

Joy cannot be held back –
it always overflows.

Joy past comprehension

Joy in living service

Praise be to the God and Father of our Lord Jesus Christ, who has blessed us in the heavenly realms with every spiritual blessing in Christ. For he chose us in him before the creation of the world to be holy and blameless in his sight. In love he predestined us to be adopted as his sons through Jesus Christ, in accordance with his pleasure and will – to the praise of his glorious grace, which he has freely given us in the One he loves. In him we have redemption through his blood, the forgiveness of sins, in accordance with the riches of God's grace that he lavished on us with all wisdom and understanding.

The joy of being part of God's plan

In this letter addressed to the young church at Ephesus, Paul expresses his amazement at ever being called to be part of God's family and to his service. He is full of praise to God for what God has graciously done – right from his decision to rescue us, however unattractive we might have been, to his promise that we shall share the future destiny of all things. It is this conviction of being part of God's plan which gives the Christian the fullest joy. When our life and work are given to God, everything we do has meaning and purpose. As we realise this, our hearts overflow with joy in God's service.

Ephesians 1:3–8

As God's adopted children, we share the joy of being part of his plan.

PEDAL for HEALTH
THIS RAINCOAT
STOPS AT ALL
INTERSECTIONS

Joy that needs expression

Joy for the world

Sing to the Lord a new song; sing to the Lord, all the earth. Sing to the Lord, praise his name; proclaim his salvation day after day. Declare his glory among the nations, his marvellous deeds among all peoples! Splendour and majesty are before him; strength and glory are in his sanctuary. O families of nations, ascribe to the Lord glory and strength!

Sing to the Lord a new song, for he has done marvellous things...Shout for joy to the Lord, all the earth, burst into jubilant song with music; make music to the Lord with the harp, with the harp and the sound of singing, with trumpets and the blast of the ram's horn – shout for joy before the Lord, the King.

The joy which must be shared

How selfish it would be if we kept this wonderful joy to ourselves! Surely it is a joy to share with all the world. We can pray that God will show us just how this can be done. Should we ask for extra training? Should we travel for him? Should we simply learn better to speak to others about what God has done for us? The first Christians, deeply grateful to God for all he had done, sang – in their hymns – of the day when 'At the name of Jesus every knee shall bow, and every tongue confess that Jesus Christ is Lord to the glory of God the Father'. That will be joy indeed! We echo this song across the centuries.

Psalm 96:1–3, 6, 7 Psalm 98:1, 4–6

Modern Hong Kong.
'Declare his marvellous deeds among all peoples!'

Joy that lasts and lasts

Joy in heaven

I heard a loud voice from the throne saying, 'Now the dwelling of God is with men, and he will live with them. They will be his people, and God himself will be with them and be their God. He will wipe every tear from their eyes. There will be no more death or mourning or crying or pain for the old order of things has passed away.'

Then I heard every creature in heaven and on earth and under the earth and on the sea, and all that is in them, singing: 'To him who sits on the throne and to the Lamb be praise and honour and glory and power, for ever and ever!'

The joy of eternity

Beyond this failing world, there is a joy which can never fail. There is a place where crying and dying are done away, where we live with God for ever, where we shall see him, and our joy will be full. There is a time when the old order of things is like a forgotten dream. Then we shall share with all God's people the privilege of praising him.

There is no joy that exceeds the joy that God gives. In that day, all the joys of earth will be one with the joys of heaven. And God will be all in all.

Revelation 21:3, 4   Revelation 5:13

The joy of eternity can be experienced now – in Christ.

A prayer of joy

O Lord of all the earth,
receive our praise
as we celebrate the wonder of your power,
as we proclaim your everlasting
faithfulness;
lift our hearts to love you more,
lift up our feeble hands to serve you better,
and lift our minds to worship you
where Jesus reigns in glory:
for you are our rejoicing here,
and our joy for all eternity.
Amen

Michael Perry

The Promise of PEACE

The promise of Peace
Peace for our lives
Peace from Christ
God's peace

Peace from God
The peace we need
Jesus, the bringer of peace

Peace that unites
Peace that puts things right with God
The price of peace

Peace that dispels fear
Peace in our consciences
The war is over

Peace past understanding
Peace in our hearts
Throughout the day

Peace for difficult times
Peace in the storm
The peace of his presence

Peace for God's people
Peace for the righteous
The way of peace

Peace that reaches out
Peace for the peacemakers
'Blessed are the peacemakers'

Peace that's active
Peace in our world
Preserving the peace

Peace that's effective
Peace in our nation
God knows best

A prayer of peace

The promise of peace

Peace for our lives

The Lord bless you and keep you; the Lord make his face shine upon you and be gracious to you; the Lord turn his face towards you and give you peace.

Peace from Christ

On the evening of that first day of the week, when the disciples were together, with the doors locked for fear of the Jews, Jesus came and stood among them and said, 'Peace be with you!' After he said this, he showed them his hands and side. The disciples were overjoyed when they saw the Lord. Again Jesus said, 'Peace be with you!'

God's peace

Peace is the quality of life and attitude of mind that we all want, but find so hard to come by. To the Hebrew of the Old Testament, it was the greatest blessing from God; Jewish people still greet each other with the word 'Peace'. To the Christian, peace is truly found in Christ himself. The Lord Jesus Christ is the bringer of peace. Before he appeared to them, the disciples had been confused and afraid. His appearance, after his resurrection from the dead, calmed their hearts and filled them with confidence and joy.

Numbers 6:24–26 John 20:19, 20, 21

'The Lord turn his face towards you and give you peace.'

Peace from God

The peace we need

The rising sun will come to us from heaven to shine on those living in darkness and in the shadow of death, to guide our feet into the path of peace

We considered him stricken by God smitten by him, and afflicted. But he was pierced for our transgressions, he was crushed for our iniquities; the punishment that brought us peace was upon him.

Christ Jesus came and preached peace to you who were far away, and peace for those who were near. For through him we both have access to the Father by one Spirit.

Jesus, the bringer of peace

In his days on earth, Jesus brought peace to all those he met – troubled as many of them were with mental anxiety and physical ailments. But his peace is of wider significance. It was promised that Jesus would bring peace to our lives too by giving us the hope of rescue and forgiveness. His peace is ours if we trust him. In Jesus, God can reach us even in our blackest moments. And no longer do we need to feel guilty, for Jesus has died to free us from the dreadful penalties of our sin. He bore them in our place as he died on the cross. So all, through God's Holy Spirit, can approach God the Father in peace.

Luke 1:78 Isaiah 53:4, 5 Ephesians 2:17, 18

No-one need remain in darkness.
God offers light and peace.

Peace that unites

Peace that puts things right with God

In Christ Jesus, you who once were far away have been brought near through the blood of Christ. For he himself is our peace.

God was pleased through Christ to reconcile to himself all things, whether things on earth or things in heaven, by making peace through his blood, shed on the cross. Once, you were alienated from God and were enemies in your minds because of your evil behaviour. But now he has reconciled you by Christ's physical body through death to present you holy in his sight, without blemish and free from accusation.

The price of peace

When we disobey God we effectively declare war on him. In all justice he cannot disregard this revolt against his sovereignty. The prophets of the Old Testament warn us continually of the consequences of defying – or ignoring – our heavenly Lord and Creator. Only as we look at Jesus do we begin to realise how much danger we are in, and how far we have come from the safe haven of the peace of God. Because of this we are open to the attacks of evil and death. But, through Christ's death, the gulf between us and God has gone. Through his sacrifice on the cross, we are brought back to him – and not only us. For through Christ, God will extend his eventual peace to all creation.

Ephesians 2:13, 14 Colossians 1:19–22

The cross of Christ is the price of our peace.

Peace that dispels fear

Peace in our consciences

You will keep in perfect peace him whose mind is steadfast, because he trusts in you. Trust in the Lord for ever, for the Lord, the Lord, is the Rock eternal.

Since we have been justified through faith we have peace with God through our Lord Jesus Christ, through whom we have gained access by faith into this grace in which we now stand. And we rejoice in the hope of the glory of God.

This then is how we know that we belong to the truth, and how we set our hearts at rest in his presence whenever our hearts condemn us. For God is greater than our hearts, and he knows everything. And this is how we know that he lives in us: we know it by the Spirit he gave us.

The war is over

Though mentally we might be persuaded that we are now secure in God's favour, in our hearts we tend to go on doubting it. It has to be brought home to us again and again that facts are more important than feelings. God's reputation is unshakable, his act of grace in Christ cannot be gainsayed. He knows better than we do, and his faithfulness is far more certain than our feelings at any time. These men of God assure us: we do have his peace. If we trust him our peace will be complete.

Isaiah 26:3, 4 Romans 5:1, 2 1 John 3:19, 20, 24

Lord, you give perfect peace . . .
to those who trust in you.

Peace past understanding

Peace in our hearts

The Lord is near. Do not be anxious about anything, but in everything, by prayer and petition with thanksgiving, present your requests to God. And the peace of God, which transcends all understanding, will guard your hearts and your minds in Christ Jesus.

You are a shield around me, O Lord, my Glorious One, who lifts up my head. To the Lord I cry aloud, and he answers me from his holy hill. I lie down and sleep; I wake again because the Lord sustains me.

I will lie down and sleep in peace, for you alone, O Lord, make me dwell in safety.

Throughout the day

All our ways we shall commit to him, all our problems leave in his hands, and rest in his peace. Unbroken contact with God, whatever happens, brings its own rewards. In times of difficulty, pain, sorrow and apprehensiveness – when it is logical to be anxious – we may nevertheless know the peace of God, which is beyond our logic. The unconquerable power of Jesus Christ will guard our hearts and minds.

Philippians 4:5–7 Psalm 3:3–5 Psalm 4:8

'Do not be anxious about anything – the peace of God will guard your hearts and your minds in Christ Jesus.'

London

The peace of God will guard your hearts and your minds in Christ Jesus.

Peace for difficult times

Peace in the storm

A furious squall came up, and the waves broke over the boat, so that it was nearly swamped. The disciples woke Jesus and said to him, 'Teacher, don't you care if we drown?' He got up, rebuked the wind and said to the waves, 'Quiet! Be Still!' Then the wind died down and it was completely calm.

Jesus said, 'The Counsellor, the Holy Spirit, whom the Father will send in my name, will teach you all things and will remind you of everything I have said to you. Peace I leave with you; my peace I give you. I do not give to you as the world gives. Do not let your hearts be troubled and do not be afraid.

The peace of his presence

Here are two episodes from the life of Jesus. In the first, the disciples are afraid. For a moment they have forgotten that they can come to no harm with Jesus close by. He seems to be ignoring them, and they wonder if he really cares. But his power is demonstrated when they cry to him.

In the second episode, Jesus promises this presence to the first Christians. They will face the storms of life as before, but he will still be close by them through his Holy Spirit.

Mark 4:37–39 John 14:26–27

'Peace I give to you. Do not let your hearts be troubled and do not be afraid.'

Peace for God's people

Peace for the righteous

Refrain from anger and turn from wrath; do not fret – it leads only to evil. For evil men will be cut off, but those who hide in the Lord will inherit the land. A little while, and the wicked will be no more, though you look for them, they will not be found. But the meek will inherit the land and enjoy great peace.

Consider the blameless, observe the upright; there is a future for the man of peace. But all sinners will be destroyed, the future of the wicked will be cut off. The salvation of the righteous comes from the Lord; he is their stronghold in time of trouble.

The way of peace

Here are our instructions for a truly peaceful life. We may look at evil people, see their success and sometimes envy them. But, at the end of the day, it is the blameless who achieve peace of heart. We shall be shocked and surprised at the suddenness of God's action against the wicked. They have nowhere to go in their time of trouble; but always we have the peace of the Lord.

Psalm 37:8–11 Psalm 37:37–39

'The meek will inherit the land and enjoy great peace.'

Peace that reaches out

Peace for the peacemakers

Jesus said, 'Salt is good, but if it loses its saltiness, how can you make it salty again? Have salt in yourselves, and be at peace with each other.'

There is deceit in the hearts of those who plot evil, but joy for those who promote peace.

Jesus said, 'Blessed are the peacemakers, for they will be called the sons of God.'

'Blessed are the peacemakers'

Through us, God will reach others with his peace. We shall have great satisfaction in this service. Surely there can be no joy greater than that of seeing others find lasting peace and happiness in the knowledge of God – especially if God has been so good as to offer them that peace through us.

This makes our responsibility very great: as God's representatives, we must be peaceful and peaceable ourselves. Too many people in our day simply *talk* peace. Speeches and marches alone are unconvincing. People who take action to bring healing and comfort to strife-torn areas of the world should command our greatest respect. The word 'peace-maker', as Matthew uses it, is really 'peace-doer'. Blessed are those who are not merely *saying*, but also *doing* something about peace – starting from home!

Mark 9:50 Proverbs 12:20 Matthew 5:9

Through us God will reach others with his peace.

Peace that's active

Peace in our world

For though we live in the world, we do not wage war as the world does. The weapons we fight with are not the weapons of the world. On the contrary, they have divine power to demolish strongholds.

Where you have envy and selfish ambition, there you find disorder and every evil practice. But the wisdom that comes from heaven is first of all pure; then peace-loving, considerate, submissive, full of mercy and good fruit, impartial and sincere. Peacemakers who sow in peace raise a harvest of righteousness.

Preserving the peace

Our responsibility goes further than *living* in peace. For the world is God's world and we – as his children – have a duty towards it: to ensure that love, peace and justice prevail. For this reason we must pray for wisdom and humility, we must learn obedience to God and develop compassion and a good and generous spirit. There are many passages in the New Testament which enjoin humility and peaceful deference to one another. Statesmen would do well to study them. We may think that only politicians have the power to influence world events. That is not true. Individual Christians down the centuries – many of them neither statesman nor politician – have influenced for good the course of world events. Their secret? – the spiritual peace-weapon of prayer.

2 Corinthians 10:3, 4 James 3:16–18

Every Christian should influence the world for peace.

Peace that's effective

Peace in our nation

This is what the Lord says – 'I am the Lord your God, who teaches you what is best for you, who directs you in the way you should go. If only you had paid attention to my commands, your peace would have been like a river.'

The fruit of righteousness will be peace; the effect of righteousness will be quietness and confidence for ever. My people will live in peaceful dwelling-places, in secure homes, in undisturbed places of rest.

God knows best

There is a sense in which a nation too, has a heart and a soul. In this respect the advice given to an individual is relevant to a nation: if there is goodness at the heart, peace breaks forth. We can help our countrymen and women to see where the secret of true peace lies. God knows what is best for them; justice and truthfulness in the nation leads to peace. We cannot reject God's commandments for ever, for he designed our world and knows us better than we know ourselves.

In diplomacy, peace concerns good relationships – not just bombs and tanks. In industry there is peace where there is also justice, fairness, security and mutual understanding, and where people can be relied upon to keep their word. There is peace in a community when people are honest about each other and recognise selfishness as the real enemy

Isaiah 48:17, 18 Isaiah 31:17, 18

Justice and truthfulness among nations leads to peace.

A prayer of peace

Lord,
make me an instrument of your peace:
where there is hatred, let me sow love,
where there is injury, forgiveness;
where there is doubt, faith;
where there is despair, hope;
where there is darkness, light;
where there is sadness, joy,
now and always,
Amen.

Traditional

The Promise of HOPE

The promise of hope

A living hope

Praise be to the God and Father of our Lord Jesus Christ! In his great mercy he has given us new birth into a living hope through the resurrection of Jesus Christ from the dead.

For what I received I passed on to you as of first importance: that Christ died for our sins according to the Scriptures, that he was buried, that he was raised on the third day according to the Scriptures, and that he appeared to Peter, and then to the Twelve. After that, he appeared to more than five hundred of the brothers at the same time.

Based on fact

The Christian hope is not just a theory – it is based on fact. Christ's resurrection is well-attested. The immediate human affects of that earth-shattering event are recorded even by non-Christian historians. And there's more: Christians today experience the power in their lives of the risen Lord Jesus Christ. Miracles did not stop at the end of the Bible. Our hope is not unfounded; it is based on fact – yet in such a way as to require a response of faith from the heart.

1 Peter 1:3 1 Corinthians 15:3–6

'He has given us new birth into a living hope.'

Hope that is permanent

A hope of life to come

We know that the one who raised the Lord Jesus from the dead will also raise us with Jesus and will bring us with you in his presence.

Brothers, we do not want you to be ignorant about those who fall asleep, or to grieve like the rest of men, who have no hope. We believe that Jesus died and rose again and so we believe that God will bring with Jesus those who have fallen asleep in him. And so we will be with the Lord for ever. Therefore encourage each other with these words.

What the resurrection means

The implications of the resurrection of Jesus Christ are dramatic. If God is so minded, he can do to us what he did to Jesus; he can raise us to life in heaven. And the Christian message is that God does indeed intend to do this for us because he loves us. Proof? Look no further than his love expressed in sending Jesus to die for us. We shall see him and each other again, says St Paul. Therefore there need be no grief, but much joy and encouragement.

2 Corinthians 4:14   1 Thessalonians 4:13, 14, 17, 18

Christ's resurrection inspires us to persevere.

Hope with good reason

Our hope is as strong as God's love

We know that in all things God works for the good of those who love him, who have been called according to his purpose. What, then, shall we say in response to this? If God is for us, who can be against us? He who did not spare his own Son, but gave him up for us all – how will he not also, along with him, graciously give us all things? Who shall separate us from the love of Christ? Shall trouble or hardship or persecution or famine or nakedness or danger or sword? I am convinced that neither death nor life, neither angels nor demons, neither the present nor the future, nor any powers, neither height nor depth, nor anything else in all creation, will be able to separate us from the love of God that is in Christ Jesus our Lord.

Our hope is sure

Paul, the great missionary traveller, states his faith in the God he could not escape. God's love was so strong that he knew it would follow him to the end of the world.

Paul emphasises God's love for all of us who serve him. How much he must love us is demonstrated in what Jesus did for us. Nothing could possibly change God's love now. Our hope is sure: his love will follow us always.

Romans 8:28–39 selection

'. . . nothing will be able to separate us from the love of God.'

Hope in the living God

Our hope is as great as God's promise

Jesus said, 'Do not let your hearts be troubled. Trust in God; trust also in me. In my Father's house are many rooms; if it were not so, I would have told you. I am going there to prepare a place for you. And if I go and prepare a place for you, I will come back and take you to be with me that you also may be where I am.'

This is a trustworthy saying that deserves full acceptance; that we have put our hope in the living God, who is the saviour of all men, and especially of those who believe.

God deserves to be trusted

Jesus' disciples need assurance. Despite all Jesus has taught them, and despite his determination to complete his mission to the world, they are unsure of what will happen to them. They begin to ask questions about the way to heaven. As he often does, Jesus explains with a picture in words.

Jesus' picture of heaven is of a great house with many rooms – enough for everyone. And the word translated 'rooms' means 'resting-places'. The same word was used for shelters along the way for weary travellers. This is Jesus' assurance – especially to the tired and despondent traveller in this life – that God will make provision for rest and refreshment. It's God's promise, and we must believe him.

John 14:1–3 1 Timothy 4:9, 10

Victoria Falls.
God's promises are sure.

Hope that's eternal

Our hope is permanent

Jesus said, 'All that the Father gives me will come to me, and whoever comes to me I will never drive away. For I have come down from heaven not to do my will but to do the will of him who sent me. And this is the will of him who sent me, that I shall lose none of all that he has given me, but raise them up at the last day. For my Father's will is that everyone who looks to the Son and believes in him shall have eternal life, and I will raise him up at the last day.'

He will keep you strong to the end, so that you will be blameless on the day of our Lord Jesus Christ. God, who has called you into fellowship with his Son Jesus Christ our Lord, is faithful.

To him who is able to keep you from falling and to present you before his glorious presence without fault and with great joy – to the only God our Saviour be glory, majesty, power and authority, through Jesus Christ our Lord, before all ages, now and for evermore! Amen.

Lasting hope

Jesus is very well aware that we will sometimes drift away from him – after all, he describes us as sheep! But he does insist that he will never *drive* us away, and that as our good shepherd he will look after us. So we can be sure that he will keep us his own to the very end. Faith and fellowship are the keys to confident hope. We must continually trust him and involve ourselves in fellowship with other Christians.

John 6:37–40 1 Corinthians 1:8, 9 Jude 24, 25

'He will keep you strong to the end.'

'You care for the land and water it; you enrich it abundantly.'

Hope that's victorious

How it will happen

Listen, I tell you a mystery: we will not all sleep, but we will all be changed – in a flash, in the twinkling of an eye, at the last trumpet. For the trumpet will sound, the dead will be raised imperishable, and we will be changed. For the perishable must clothe itself with the imperishable, and the mortal with immortality. When the perishable has been clothed with the imperishable, and the mortal with immortality, then the saying that is written will come true: 'Death has been swallowed up in victory.' 'Where, O death, is your victory? Where, O death, is your sting?' The sting of death is sin, and the power of sin is the law. But thanks be to God! He gives us the victory through our Lord Jesus Christ.

Hope springs its surprise

Heaven is going to happen very suddenly, says St Paul. Again, it's a picture that he is using – heaven defies description, and so do the events of the Christian hope. We mustn't be put off by his wonderfully colourful language. This is what he means: it's going to be like waking up, like lightning, faster than it takes to blink, like a trumpet sounding. The life to come will be like the real us getting dressed in a new immortal body when this mortal body has perished away.

1 Corinthians 15:51–57

'The life to come will be like the real us getting dressed in a new immortal body.'

Hope with a future

Pictures of hope

Then I, John, saw a new heaven and a new earth, for the first heaven and the first earth had passed away, and there was no longer any sea. I saw the Holy City, the new Jerusalem, coming down out of heaven from God, prepared as a bride beautifully dressed for her husband. And I heard a loud voice from the throne saying, 'Now the dwelling of God is with men, and he will live with them. They will be his people, and God himself will be with them and be their God.' He said to me: 'It is done. I am the Alpha and the Omega, the Beginning and the End. To him who is thirsty I will give to drink without cost from the spring of the water of life. He who overcomes will inherit all this, and I will be his God and he will be my son.'

For here we do not have an enduring city, but we are looking for the city that is to come.

Hope looks forward

The writers of 'Revelation' and 'Hebrews' picture heaven as a beautiful city. It is as though we are travellers – tired, weary and thirsty – like the people of Israel struggling through the desert towards their promised land. And there, on the horizon, is the sight of a beautiful city. What wonderful relief, what glory, and what celebration!

Revelation 21:1–3, 6, 7 Hebrews 13:14

The New Jerusalem – 'A bride beautifully dressed for her husband.'

Hope with no regrets

False hopes

When men tell you to consult mediums and spiritists, who whisper and mutter, should not a people enquire of their God? Why consult the dead on behalf of the living? To the law and to the testimony! If they do not speak according to this word, they have no light of dawn.

Do not practise divination or sorcery. Do not turn to mediums or seek out spiritists, for you will be defiled by them, I am the Lord your God.

Let no-one be found among you . . . who is a medium or spiritist or who consults the dead. Anyone who does these things is detestable to the Lord. You must be blameless before the Lord your God.

Diviners see visions that lie, they tell dreams that are false. They give comfort in vain.

Beware spiritism

Don't travel this way because it leads to disappointment — and worse. Suddenly, there is a sombre note for people who follow false hopes. And it's only right that we should be warned. Many who have lost loved ones try to follow them by using mediums or séances. At the end of this road there is no heavenly city, but only danger. Besides which, the Bible says explicitly that we are not to follow it. God has provided Christ to be our hope; to follow any other way is to reject his provision and his will.

Isaiah 8:19–20 Leviticus 19:26, 31 Deuteronomy 18:9–14 selection Zechariah 10:2

Following false hope brings disappointment.

Hope that enriches

Hope here and now

I pray also that the eyes of your heart may be enlightened in order that you may know the hope to which he has called you, the riches of his glorious inheritance in the saints, and his incomparably great power for us who believe. That power is like the working of his mighty strength, which he exerted in Christ when he raised him from the dead and seated him at his right hand in the heavenly realms, far above all rules and authority, power and dominion, and every title that can be given, not only in the present age but also in the one to come. And God placed all things under his feet and appointed him to be head over everything for the church.

Now to him who is able to do immeasurably more than all we ask or imagine, according to his power that is at work within us, to him be glory in the church and in Christ Jesus throughout all generations, for ever and ever! Amen.

Start right away

We completely misunderstand the Christian faith if we think it is *only* concerned with heaven. The very same power that God demonstrated in Christ is available for us here and now. For God has raised him to be Lord of all. So Christianity is not a bequest from a dead saviour, but a shared inheritance with a living Lord. His power to live our lives is already there for the asking: the power to serve him in this world, the power to win others to know and love him. Given this hope, we can start right away.

Ephesians 1:18–22 Ephesians 3:20, 21

'To him be glory in Christ Jesus for ever and ever!'

Hope that inspires

Look up

Do not let your hands hang limp. The Lord your God is with you, he is mighty to save. He will take great delight in you, he will quiet you with his love, he will rejoice over you with singing.

Let us throw off everything that hinders and the sin that so easily entangles, and let us run with perseverance the race marked out for us. Let us fix our eyes on Jesus, the author and perfector of our faith, who for the joy set before him endured the cross, scorning its shame, and sat down at the right hand of the throne of God.

All this is for your benefit, so that the grace that is reaching more and more people may cause thanksgiving to overflow to the glory of God. Therefore we do not lose heart. Though outwardly we are wasting away, yet inwardly we are being renewed day by day.

Therefore, strengthen your feeble arms and weak knees! Make level paths for your feet, so that the lame may not be disabled but rather healed.

Never lose heart

With the prospect of heaven and the encouragement of Christ's resurrection power to help us on our way, we need never lose heart. God can rescue us out of any difficult situation that we might meet. He takes an interest in everything we do; he gives us his peace and we enter into his joy.

Not even the passing of the years can depress us, for the Spirit of the great Creator is within us – leading us on to new and better things. Hope in Christ, and do not be dismayed!

Zephaniah 3:16, 17 Hebrews 12:1, 2 2 Corinthians 4:15–16 Hebrews 12:12, 13

Looking to Jesus 'We mount up with wings like eagles.'

A prayer of hope

Our mighty Lord and Saviour,
the hope of all mankind:
we trust you,
we trust your promises,
we trust your mercy and your love;
we trust you because we have seen you in Jesus
and we know that you are faithful.
Be the Lord of our lives,
the joy of our hearts
and the hope of all our days.
Amen

Michael Perry

The Promise of
LIFE

The promise of life

Life's beginnings

And the Lord God formed man from the dust of the ground and breathed into his nostrils the breath of life, and man became a living being.

This is what the Sovereign Lord says to these bones: I will make breath enter you, and you will come to life. I will attach tendons to you and make flesh come upon you and cover you with skin. O my people, I am going to open your graves and bring you up from them … Then you, my people, will know that I am the Lord, when I open your graves and bring you up from them. I will put my spirit in you and you will live.

The giver of life

The Old Testament has a way of describing the beginning of human life. It is a picture that expresses the fact of God's initiative in giving us life: God breathes into us the breath of life. Without him we are only dust. The Prophet Ezekiel picks up this same picture to give hope to his people. Where there is failure and death – Ezekiel's dry bones – there can be hope and a new beginning if God breathes in, 'inspires', his own life.

We may think all hope is gone; God is telling us that he can yet breathe life into the wreckage of our failures. For God is life-from-death, and hope-out-of-hopelessness.

Genesis 2:7 Ezekiel 37:5, 6, 12–14

'I will make breath enter you, and you will come to life.'

Life with a purpose

Life's realities

The Lord brings death and makes alive; he brings down to the grave and raises up. The Lord sends poverty and wealth; he humbles and exalts. He raises the poor from the dust and lifts the needy from the ash heap; he seats them with princes and has them inherit a throne of honour.

We brought nothing into the world, and we can take nothing out of it.

Job fell to the ground in worship and said, 'Naked I came from my mother's womb, and naked I shall depart. The Lord gave and the Lord has taken away; may the Name of the Lord be praised!'

A life that is conscious of God

People are very careful not to speak too much of death – as if it were a forbidden subject. But a little realism about life and death makes us aware of how very dependent upon God we are. In modern society, we get lost in our money-making and pursuit of personal pleasure. We forget that God has the final say. It would take only a decision of his to reduce all our ambitions to nothing. We can take nothing out of this world when we die, but we can leave something of lasting value behind. So, to those who seek him, God promises a life of significance in his service – even though it be a life of sacrifice too – for we shall be taking part in his plan.

1 Samuel 2:6–8 1 Timothy 6:7 Job 1:20–21

'We brought nothing into the world and can take nothing out of it.'

Life that comes from God

Life's new birth

Jesus said, 'I tell you the truth, unless a man is born of water and the Spirit, he cannot enter the kingdom of God. Flesh gives birth to flesh, but the Spirit gives birth to Spirit. You should not be surprised at my saying, "You must be born again." The wind blows wherever it pleases. You hear it sound, but you cannot tell where it comes from or where it is going. So it is with everyone born of the Spirit. The Son of Man must be lifted up, that everyone who believes may have eternal life in him. For God so loved the world that he gave his one and only Son, that whoever believes in him shall not perish but have eternal life.'

Spiritual life

In this passage from St John's Gospel Jesus speaks about a new kind of life: being born over again. This is not a physical birth explains Jesus. It has more to do with trusting in God, belief expressed in baptism, possession by the Holy Spirit and entry into the kingdom of God.

It's an intangible thing – you can't see it happening. It's like the wind, invisible save for its effects. But this new-born life is real all the same, and has visible effects upon all who find it.

John 3:5–8, 14–16

'You must be born again.'

Life that overflows

Life's new power

And afterwards, I will pour out my Spirit on all people. On my servants, both men and women, I will pour out my Spirit in those days.

On the evening of that first day of the week, when the disciples were together, with the doors locked for fear of the Jews, Jesus came and stood among them and said, 'Peace be with you! As the Father has sent me, I am sending you.' And with that he breathed on them and said, 'Receive the Holy Spirit.'

When the day of Pentecost came, they were all together in one place. Suddenly a sound like the blowing of a violent wind came from heaven and filled the whole house where they were sitting. All of them were filled with the Holy Spirit and began to speak in other tongues as the Spirit enabled them.

If the Spirit of him who raised Jesus from the dead is living in you, he who raised Christ from the dead will also give life to your mortal bodies through his Spirit, who lives in you.

The Lord of life

The great founding events of the early church were the resurrection of Jesus from the dead, and the coming of the Holy Spirit to his disciples.

The Christian church still has the same commission today, still the same power of life. It may be thwarted by antiquated forms, but spirit-energised life is no less available to Christians who believe and claim it. The Spirit of God who raised Jesus from the dead is living in us!

Joel 2:28, 29 John 20:19, 21, 22 Acts 2:1, 2, 4 Romans 8:11

The Holy Spirit – life's new power.

Life that's immortal

Life's new hope

Don't you know that all of us who were baptised into Christ Jesus were baptised into his death? We were therefore buried with him through baptism into death in order that, just as Christ was raised from the dead through the glory of the Father, we too may live a new life. If we have been united with him in his death, we will certainly also be united with him in his resurrection.

When you were dead in your sins and in the uncircumcision of your sinful nature, God made you alive with Christ. He forgave us all our sins, having cancelled the written code, with its regulations, that was against us and that stood opposed to us; he took it away, nailing it to the cross.

Life out of death!

Our baptism is the symbol of our spiritual death and life – in that order. Paul's comparison is this: As Jesus came to die to release us, so we must become dead to the dominance of sin. As Jesus rose to new life so, as part of him, we too can rise – to new spiritual life now, and eternal life in the world to come. God has made us alive with Christ! As far as God's law is concerned, we have failed it and are condemned to death. But Christ comes to rescue us! By his death he takes away the power of sin to kill. By rising to life again he brings us new life.

Romans 6:3–5 Colossians 2:13, 14

'As Jesus rose to new life so, as part of him, we too can rise.'

*Life's potential is fulfilled
through faith in God.*

Life that's full and free

Life's greatest adventure

Jesus said, 'I am the way, the truth, and the life, no one comes to the Father except through me.

God has given us new birth into a living hope through the resurrection of Jesus Christ from the dead, and into an inheritance that can never perish, spoil or fade – kept in heaven for you, who through faith are shielded by God's power until the coming of salvation that is ready to be revealed in the last time.

Jesus said, 'I have come that they might have life, and have it to the full.'

Life here and hereafter

Now we see the dimensions of the life which Jesus gives. It is the life which brings us to God. No discipline or mere philosophy will do that.

This new spiritual life is available to us on earth and in heaven. Here, it is full and free; there, it is certain and incorruptible. Peter describes it as 'an inheritance', something rich and wonderful by God's provision.

Sometimes religious people give the impression that Christianity is only about heaven. At other times, heaven doesn't get a mention. The truth is: it's about both! God's life never dies. And, if he lives in us now through our faith in Jesus, then he will carry us triumphantly through this world and on into the eternal joy of living by his side.

John 14:6   1 Peter 1:3, 4, 5   John 10:10

Jesus said, 'I have come that they might have life, and have it to the full.'

Life that's confident

Life's assured future

Jesus said, 'My sheep listen to my voice; I know them, and they follow me. I give them eternal life, and they shall never perish; no one can snatch them out of my hand. My Father, who has given them to me, is greater than all; no one can snatch them out of my Father's hand. I and the Father are one.

This is the testimony: God has given us eternal life, and this life is in his Son. He who has the Son has life; he who does not have the Son of God does not have life. I write these things to you who believe in the Name of the Son of God so that you may know that you have eternal life.

Being sure of life

Sometimes our despondent feelings get the better of us. We find ourselves looking at the bad side of this world, and we wonder if anything happier and better can ever be. The more humble we are and the more we feel undeserving, the greater difficulty we have in believing that God's eternal life can really be for us. John gives us two clear promises:

1 Jesus our shepherd will never let even one of his sheep be snatched away from him.
2 If Jesus is our Lord, we do have eternal life.

John 10:27–30 1 John 5:11–13

Christian peace is the result of confidence in the promises of God.

Life that's strong

Life's source of strength

Jesus said, 'I am the true vine and my Father is the gardener. He cuts off every branch in me that bears no fruit, while every branch that does bear fruit he trims clean so that it will be even more fruitful. Remain in me, and I will remain in you. No branch can bear fruit by itself; it must remain in the vine. Neither can you bear fruit unless you remain in me. I am the vine; you are the branches. If a man remains in me and I in him, he will bear much fruit; apart from me you can do nothing. If you remain in me and my words remain in you, ask whatever you wish, and it will be given you. This is to my Father's glory, that you bear much fruit, showing yourselves to be my disciples. You did not choose me, but I chose you to go and bear fruit – fruit that will last.'

Cling to life!

Jesus reminds us that good intentions are not enough. We must stay close to him. He gives us the picture of the vine – a very old Hebrew picture of the people of God.

Throughout the winter, the branches of the vine appear dead; you might be forgiven for pruning them off! But the truth is that as long as they are attached to the stem, the leaves and the fruit will be there in the summer. Jesus is saying that we must stay close to him – above all in prayer and study of his word. As the branches draw strength from the vine in order to bear grapes, so we can bear fruit in our lives by drawing strength from him.

John 15:1, 2, 4, 5, 7, 8, 16

Jesus said, 'I chose you to go and bear fruit.'

Life that's fruitful

Life's choices

Listen to a father's instruction; pay attention and gain understanding. I give you sound learning, so do not forsake my teaching. Lay hold of my words with all your heart; keep my commands and you will live.

Those who live according to the sinful nature have their minds set on what that nature desires; but those who live in accordance with the Spirit have their minds set on what the Spirit desires. The mind of sinful man is death, but the mind controlled by the Spirit is life and peace.

Do not be deceived: God cannot be mocked. A man reaps what he sows. The one who sows to please his sinful nature, from that nature will reap destruction; the one who sows to please the Spirit, from the Spirit will reap eternal life.

Plan for a useful life

The Christian faith is absolutely realistic when it comes to psychology. The ideas we plant in our minds may be hidden for a while, but eventually they come out into the open and affect the way we speak and act. That is why it is so important to let the Holy Spirit be the source of our ideas and to influence all our thinking. Paul says it's like the harvest: if you sow good seed, given the right conditions you'll get a good crop. 'Sow to please the Spirit,' he says. The thinking and praying we do, as we reflect on God's truths and all that is beautiful and honourable, will finally emerge in a God-like character and a life which honours him.

Proverbs 4:1, 2, 4 Romans 8:5, 6 Galatians 6:7, 8

The mind controlled by the Spirit of life and peace.

Life that's satisfying

Life's full stature

Like newborn babies, crave pure spiritual milk, so that by it you may grow up in your salvation.

I gave you milk, not solid food, for you were not yet ready for it. Indeed you are still not ready.

Then Jesus declared, 'I am the bread of life. He who comes to me will never go hungry, and he who believes in me will never be thirsty . . . I am the living bread that came down from heaven. If a man eats of this bread he will live for ever. This bread is my flesh, which I will give for the life of the world.'

Feed your life, use your life

In these three passages Peter, Paul and John use the same idea in different ways. The idea is feeding – feeding our lives. When we first become believers in Christ, we find it very difficult to take in deep and complicated doctrine. At this stage the main thing is for us to grow strong and independent of those who first taught us. But, as Paul points out, if we don't grow up in the Christian life – if we still can take only milk as the years go by – we risk becoming stunted in our growth as Christians. We must feed solidly on Christian teachings, ready and asking for instruction. We must leave the squabbling of infancy behind us. At every stage of our needs, Jesus is able to provide. He is the 'bread of life'.

1 Peter 2:2 1 Corinthians 3:2 John 6:35, 51

Faith in God is the key to life and spiritual growth.

A prayer for life

Spirit of Life,
breathe into us
your love, your joy, your devotion;
your energy, your purity,
your wisdom and your power;
so that, dead as we are,
in Christ we may live:
to the glory of God the Father.
Amen.

Michael Perry

The Promise of Forgiveness

The promise of forgiveness

Our prayer and God's answer

Have mercy on me O God, according to your unfailing love; according to your great compassion blot out my transgressions. Wash away all my iniquity and cleanse me from my sin.

Peter replied, 'Repent and be baptised, every one of you, in the name of Jesus Christ so that your sins may be forgiven. And you will receive the gift of the Holy Spirit. The promise is for you and your children and for all who are far off – for all whom the Lord our God will call.'

'Come now, let us reason together,' says the Lord. 'Though your sins are like scarlet, they shall be as white as snow; though they are red as crimson, they shall be like wool.'

The need for forgiveness

The Christian symbol of God's mercy is baptism. Baptism represents *the washing away of our sin*. It is a living picture. Water itself can't wash away sin: God can through Jesus Christ. Sometimes it is hard for us to admit that we really need forgiveness at all. We feel almost insulted when Christian preachers say that everyone has sinned. This is because we are thinking of great big deliberate sins, and they are thinking of our every-day sorts of failure too. Sin, in the Bible, means simply 'missing the mark'. We fall short of God's great standard for his creation – some of us fall a lot shorter than others!

Psalm 51:1, 2   Acts 2:38–40   Isaiah 1:18

Wash me and I shall be whiter than snow.

Forgiveness to meet our need

Facing facts

All have sinned and fall short of the glory of God.

If we claim to be without sin, we deceive ourselves and the truth is not in us. If we confess our sins, he is faithful and just and will forgive us our sins and purify us from all unrighteousness. If we claim we have not sinned, we make him out to be a liar and his word has no place in our lives.

He who conceals his sins does not prosper, but whoever confesses and renounces them finds mercy. Blessed is the man who always fears the Lord, but he who hardens his heart falls into trouble.

The truth about forgiveness

The New Testament is absolutely realistic as far as our condition before God is concerned. God has spoken – he says we are sinners – and that alone should be enough to make us think.

People differ: some feel guilty for the slightest reason. If you are like this, remember God's forgiveness is readily available when you own up to him and admit your failure. Others don't like hearing about sin – they don't feel 'sinners'. If this is you, then ask yourself, 'What am I doing with Jesus?'. To reject him, to disobey him – that is sin.

Romans 3:23 1 John 1:8–10 Proverbs 28:13, 14

All fall short of God's standard.

Forgiveness for the asking

Act now

Seek the Lord while he may be found; call on him while he is near. Let the wicked forsake his way and the evil man his thoughts. Let him turn to the Lord, and he will have mercy on him, and to our God, for he will freely pardon.

Rend your heart and not your garments. Return to the Lord your God, for he is gracious and compassionate, slow to anger, and abounding in love, and he relents from sending calamity.

The opportunity for forgiveness

Coupled with the promises of forgiveness in these passages there's a great urgency. Opportunities to sort things out with God come and quickly pass by. Of course it's only our imagination, but God seems very near sometimes and at other times very far away. It's when he's near, speaking indirectly to our hearts and consciences, that we can most readily turn to him and ask for his forgiveness and peace.

The Hebrew people used to make a great outward show of regret. Before God they would display their superficial repentance by tearing up the clothes they were wearing. The prophets told them that God was not impressed; it's a change of heart he wants, not a change of appearance! An occasional appearance in church may do much to satisfy our conscience, but it need not represent a real turning to God.

Isaiah 55:6, 7 Joel 2:13

Seek the Lord while he may be found.

-1767-
Let others

Forgiveness undeserved

Coming to our senses

Jesus said: 'There was a man who had two sons. The younger one said to his father, "Father, give me my share of the estate." So he divided his property between them. Not long after that the younger son got together all he had, set off for a distant country and there squandered his wealth in wild living. When he came to his senses, he said, "How many of my father's hired men have food to spare, and here I am starving to death! I will set out and go back to my father and say to him: Father, I have sinned against heaven and against you. I am no longer worthy to be called your son; make me like one of your hired men." So he got up and went to his father. But while he was still a long way off, his father saw him and was filled with compassion for him; he ran to his son, threw his arms around him and kissed him.'

The desire for forgiveness

This poignant story that Jesus told is worth close examination. It is about a young man who thought he could do without God but was forced by circumstances to change his mind. God is represented in the story by the father. Like the prodigal son, we too can change our minds and return to our heavenly Father. There's no need for us to try to work our way back to him. He wants to forgive us freely; however far away or foolish we have been, God is waiting to forgive us everything.

Luke 15:11–13, 17–20

*No matter how far we have gone,
we can return.*

Forgiveness lovingly offered

God is very merciful

The Lord is compassionate and gracious, slow to anger, abounding in love. He will not always accuse, nor will he harbour his anger for ever; he does not treat us as our sins deserve or repay us according to our iniquities. For as high as the heavens are above the earth, so great is his love for those who fear him; as far as the east is from the west, so far has he removed our transgressions from us.

'I will frown on you no longer, for I am merciful,' declares the Lord. 'I will not be angry for ever. Only acknowledge your guilt – you have rebelled against the Lord your God. Return, faithless people,' declares the Lord.

The sacrifices of God are a broken spirit; a broken and contrite heart, O God, you will not despise.

The God of forgiveness

We can be sure that God is high-minded and not devious. He is not vindictive and does not lurk there, watching for an opportunity to punish us. In a way we can scarcely understand, the sacrifice of Jesus upon the cross of Calvary has satisfied his justice. God actually wants to lift from us the heavy burden of our sin, and to remove it far away. He sees our unhappiness, and he respects it.

Though God is judge of all the earth, he is merciful and *will* forgive. His patience has not run out, however much we might have provoked him.

Psalm 103:8–12 Jeremiah 3:12, 13, 14 Psalm 51:17

'A contrite heart, O Lord,
you will not despise.'

A righteous man may have many troubles, but the Lord delivers him from them all.

Forgiveness graciously given

Our forgiveness – what it cost him

The priest is to lay both hands on the head of the live goat and confess over it all the wickedness and rebellion of the Israelites – all their sins – and put them on the goat's head. He shall send the goat away into the desert in the care of a man appointed for the task. The goat will carry on itself all their sins to a solitary place.

Surely he took up our infirmities and carried our sorrows, yet we considered him stricken by God, smitten by him, and afflicted. But he was pierced for our transgressions, he was crushed for our iniquities; the punishment that brought us peace was upon him, and by his wounds we are healed. We all, like sheep, have gone astray, each of us has turned to his own way and the Lord has laid on him the iniquity of us all.

The way of forgiveness

The 'scapegoat' wasn't a very sophisticated idea but indicates how God might deal with our sin. Far more wonderful and beautiful was the prophet Isaiah's picture of suffering for other people's sins – which itself turns out to be a poetic, but accurate, description of the sacrifice of our Lord Jesus Christ.

Read again these amazing words of Isaiah, see how they apply to Jesus, and think yourself into the picture – for he died for you.

Leviticus 16:21, 22 Isaiah 53:4–6

'He was pierced for our transgressions;
the punishment that brought us peace
was upon him.'

Forgiveness with justice

Our forgiveness – how God gives it

This righteousness from God comes through faith in Jesus Christ to all who believe. There is no difference for all have sinned and fall short of the glory of God, and are justified freely by his grace through the redemption that came by Christ Jesus. God presented him as a sacrifice of atonement, through faith in his blood.

God forgave us all our sins, having cancelled the written code, with its regulations, that was against us and that stood opposed to us; he took it away, nailing it to the cross.

The pictures of forgiveness

The great problem of talking about God is that we haven't got the words to do it, so we have to understand things through approximate human ideas. In his explanation, St Paul combines a legal idea – after all he was a trained lawyer – with an idea inherited from his Hebrew faith. We are 'justified'. It means that we are 'acquitted' as in a court of law. But more than that, we have been given a new and innocent character – that of Jesus Christ himself. We are 'redeemed', purchased back by God. Paul explains that Christ has taken the sentence of our guilt to the cross – and cancelled it. We can be forgiven.

Romans 3:22–25 Colossians 2:13, 14

God's justice is always perfect.

Forgiveness for all

Our forgiveness – how God achieved it

He himself bore our sins in his body on the tree, so that we might die to sins and live for righteousness; by his wounds you have been healed.

But if anybody does sin, we have one who speaks to the Father in our defence – Jesus Christ, the Righteous One. He is the atoning sacrifice for our sins, and not only for ours but also for the sins of the whole world.

Who will bring any charge against those whom God has chosen? It is God who justifies. Who is he that condemns? Christ Jesus, who died – more than that, who was raised to life – is at the right hand of God and is also interceding for us.

Forgiveness for us and for everyone

We look again at the cost, and the scope of the sacrifice for sin made by our Lord Jesus Christ. He was the 'righteous one', the only one without sin. He took upon himself our sins as he hung in agony on the cross. His sacrifice was 'atoning' – it made us 'at one' with God, reconciled to him. It also has implications for people of the whole wide world. Christ can be their saviour too, and we must let them know.

Most importantly, forgiveness is not only in the past. We know that in our weakness we shall fail however much we try not to. But we can go back to God through Christ and ask for his forgiveness all over again. God does not intend that Christians should get bogged down in their sin. He wants us to be free and confident so that we might tell the world the wonderful news.

1 Peter 2:24 1 John 2:1, 2 Romans 8:33, 34

Scene through an arch.
Forgiveness gives us a new hope.

Forgiveness that spreads

Forgiveness is for sharing

Peter came to Jesus and asked, 'Lord, how many times shall I forgive my brother when he sins against me? Up to seven times?' Jesus answered, 'I tell you, not seven times, but seventy-seven times.'

Our Father in heaven . . . Forgive us our debts, as we also have forgiven our debtors . . . If you forgive men when they sin against you, your heavenly Father will also forgive you.

Therefore, as God's chosen people, holy and dearly loved, clothe yourselves with compassion, kindness, humility, gentleness and patience. Bear with each other and forgive whatever grievances you may have against one another. Forgive as the Lord forgave you.

Forgiveness in Christ's family

If we don't forgive each other, we can hardly expect God to forgive us. Sometimes it takes an effort to forgive other people – but we must do it! Jesus taught us in the Lord's Prayer deliberately to forgive one another. That's what 'as we also have forgiven' means. Forgiveness is a wonderful and healing thing – in businesses, schools, communities – and especially in churches. A church, above all, must be a place of forgiveness. For how will anyone coming in, believe that God is willing to forgive us if we do not show willingness to forgive each other.

Matthew 18:21, 22 Matthew 6:9, 12, 14 Colossians 3:12, 13

As God's people, clothe yourselves with compassion, kindness, humility, gentleness, and patience.

Forgiveness the example

Jesus and Stephen

When they came to the place called The Skull there they crucified him, along with the criminals – one on his right, the other on his left. Jesus said, 'Father, forgive them, for they do not know what they are doing.'

Stephen, full of the Holy Spirit, looked up to heaven and saw the glory of God, and Jesus standing at the right hand of God. 'Look,' he said, 'I see heaven open and the Son of Man standing at the right hand of God.' At this they covered their ears and, yelling at the top of their voices, they all rushed at him, dragged him out of the city and began to stone him. Stephen prayed, 'Lord Jesus, receive my spirit.' Then he fell on his knees and cried out, 'Lord, do not hold this sin against them.'

Something to admire and copy

Here are two wonderful examples of forgiveness. And we think we have problems! We must not, as Christians, fail to forgive others for hurting us. For we must remember how much our world hurt Jesus and yet he said 'Father, forgive them, for they do not know what they are doing'. Stephen, the first Christian martyr, followed his Lord's example of forgiveness, and so must we even if we are not called to pay the supreme price for our faith.

Luke 23:33, 34 Acts 7:55–60 selection

Examples from the past should be our light for the future.

A prayer of forgiveness

Father of all,
great must be your love,
that you should send
   Jesus your Son to die
so that we might be forgiven.
What can we offer you
   but the obedience of our hearts
   and the service of our lives?
Accept our willing sacrifice.
How can we honour you
   but by forgiving
   those who have wronged us?
Accept our joyful duty,
in the name of Jesus Christ our Lord.
Amen.

Michael Perry

The Promise of Comfort

The promise of comfort
The need for comfort
Everyone's experience

Comfort that is reassuring
The God of comfort
Someone to talk to

Comfort that is tender
The Shepherd
A picture of comfort

Comfort that is trustworthy
The Promise
Treasure in heaven

Comfort that is certain
The living hope
Do you believe?

Comfort that is lasting
The end of tears
Unassailable joy

Comfort that is deep
Comfort through forgiveness
A clear conscience

Comfort that is clear
Comfort through confidence
You can trust him!

Comfort that is surprising
Comfort in suffering
The fellowship of the cross

Comfort that is satisfying
Thank you, Lord!
How wonderful is God

A prayer for comfort

The promise of comfort

The need for comfort

Even today my complaint is bitter; God's hand is heavy in spite of my groaning. If only I knew where to find him; if only I could go to his dwelling! But if I go to the east, he is not there; if I go to the west, I do not find him. When he is at work in the north, I do not see him; when he turns to the south, I catch no glimpse of him.

O God, you are my God, earnestly I seek you; my soul thirsts for you, my body longs for you, in a dry and weary land where there is no water. I have seen you in the sanctuary and beheld your power and your glory. Because your love is better than life, my lips will glorify you. I will praise you as long as I live.

Everyone's experience

No one gets through life without meeting sorrow at some point. Suddenly, we wonder what God can be doing. Where was he when we needed him? If only we could speak to him directly and challenge him to explain, then we might find some comfort. But usually at such times God seems remote. That may be because we have not ever made a practice of coming into his presence. It may be because our sorrow has led to depression, when nothing is certain – least of all God. Often, to our surprise, we can find comfort by worshipping him in the silence of a church or in the loneliness of the outside, by reading of others who suffered in the Bible, or by singing – perhaps through tears – the hymns that we know.

Job 23:2, 3, 8, 9 Psalm 63:1–4

My soul thirsts for you . . . in a dry land.

Comfort that is reassuring

The God of comfort

I cry aloud to the Lord; I lift up my voice to the Lord for mercy. I pour out my complaint before him; before him I tell my trouble. When my spirit grows faint within me, it is you who know my way.

There is no one like the God of Jeshurun, who rides on the heavens to help you and on the clouds in his majesty. The eternal God is your refuge, and underneath are the everlasting arms.

Even though I walk through the valley of the shadow of death, I will fear no evil, for you are with me; your rod and staff, they comfort me. Surely goodness and love will follow me all the days of my life, and I will dwell in the house of the Lord for ever.

Someone to talk to

Even if the conversation is rather one-sided, we can take comfort in telling God our troubles confident that he knows us and understands. The people of the Bible were clear in their conviction that though God was far beyond the heavens, yet his powerful and loving arms were near and ready to help. He is our shepherd, wrote the Psalmist. He is not afraid of the valley of the shadow. He will keep us safe until that day when we shall smile again in his presence.

Psalm 142:1–3 Deuteronomy 33:26–27 Psalm 23:4, 6

'It is you, O Lord, who knows my way.'

Comfort that is tender

The Shepherd

The Lord is my shepherd . . . he makes me lie down in green pastures, he leads me beside quiet waters, he restores my soul.

He tends his flock like a shepherd: he gathers the lambs in his arms and carries them close to his heart; he gently leads those that have young.

The Lord says, 'I myself will search for my sheep and look after them. I will search for the lost and bring back the strays. I will bind up the injured and strengthen the weak . . .'

Jesus said, 'I am the good shepherd; I know my sheep and my sheep know me – just as the Father knows me and I know the Father – and I lay down my life for the sheep.'

A picture of comfort

Again and again, the Bible returns to this theme. The shepherd treats each sheep as an individual. He knows it and he cares for it in all circumstances. He feeds, he defends, he gathers, he heals, he strengthens and he comforts.

So, if the Lord is our shepherd, we have a wonderful companion – who will do all these things. He cares, not just generally for all his people, but also individually and with peculiar tenderness for each one of us.

Psalm 23:1, 2, 3 Isaiah 40:11 Ezekiel 34:11, 16 John 10:14, 15

'He leads me beside quiet waters,
he restores my soul.'

Comfort that is trustworthy

The Promise

God so loved the world that he gave his one and only Son, that whoever believes in him shall not perish but have eternal life. For God did not send his Son into the world to condemn the world, but to save the world through him.

Do not let your hearts be troubled. Trust in God; trust also in me. In my Father's house are many rooms; if it were not so, I would have told you. I am going there to prepare a place for you. And if I go and prepare a place for you, I will come back and take you to be with me that you also may be where I am.

Praise be to the God and Father of our Lord Jesus Christ! In his great mercy he has given us new birth into a living hope through the resurrection of Jesus Christ from the dead, and into an inheritance that can never perish, spoil or fade – kept in heaven for you, who through faith are shielded by God's power.

Treasure in heaven

Here is the promise of Jesus – and the reminder of Peter – about the life that is to come. They want us to be comforted and assured that we are included in God's plans.

Peter tells us to base our hope on Jesus' resurrection from the dead. Others may have no hope, but we have. For even if we 'fall asleep', God can raise us to life again. Though life can be hard here, our treasure is in heaven.

John 3:16–17 John 14:1–3 1 Peter 1:3–5

'. . . I will come back and take you to be with me.'

Comfort that is certain

The living hope

'Lord,' Martha said to Jesus 'if you had been here, my brother would not have died.' Jesus said to her, 'Your brother will rise again.' Martha answered, 'I know he will rise again in the resurrection at the last day.' Jesus said to her, 'I am the resurrection and the life. He who believes in me will live, even though he dies; and whoever lives and believes in me will never die. Do you believe this?' 'Yes, Lord,' she told him, 'I believe that you are the Christ, the Son of God, who was to come into the world.'

Brothers, we do not want you to be ignorant about those who fall asleep, or to grieve like the rest of men, who have no hope. We believe that Jesus died and rose again and so we believe that God will bring with Jesus those who have fallen asleep in him. And so we will be with the Lord for ever. Therefore encourage each other with these words.

Do you believe?

Jesus challenges a close friend, Martha, about her faith. Does she believe in life after death? Yes, she says; she has faith for her brother. But does she have faith for herself? Jesus invites her – and us – to trust him completely.

John 11:21, 23–27 1 Thessalonians 4:13, 14, 17, 18

Trust in Christ brings comfort in the certainty of resurrection life.

The comfort of security.

Comfort that is lasting

The end of tears

Then I saw a new heaven and a new earth, for the first heaven and the first earth had passed away, and there was no longer any sea. I saw the Holy City, the New Jerusalem coming down out of heaven from God, prepared as a bride beautifully dressed for her husband. And I heard a loud voice from the throne saying. 'Now the dwelling of God is with men, and he will live with them. They will be his people, and God himself will be with them and be their God. He will wipe every tear from their eyes. There will be no more death or mourning or crying or pain, for the old order of things has passed away.'

Jesus said, 'Now is your time of grief, but I will see you again and you will rejoice, and no one will take away your joy.'

Unassailable joy

The final intervention of God to save us from our troubles is represented by the descent from the skies of a beautiful city — a new home for us all. This is the wedding of God and his people; for he comes to live with us at last.

But the end is not yet, and we have to live in the present. Jesus says that Christians will go through time of bitter sorrow and disappointment. But, through the comfort of the Holy Spirit, deep down is an unassailable joy. For, as St Paul says, 'we are citizens of heaven'.

Revelation 21:1–4 John 16:22

For the Christian there is an unassailable joy which will last beyond time itself.

Comfort that is deep

Comfort through forgiveness

Blessed is he whose transgressions are forgiven, whose sins are covered. Blessed is the man whose sin the Lord does not count against him and in whose spirit is no deceit. When I kept silent, my bones wasted away through my groaning all day long. Then I acknowledged my sin to you and did not cover up my iniquity. I said, 'I will confess my transgressions to the Lord' – and you forgave the guilt of my sin.

I will praise you, O Lord. Although you were angry with me, your anger has turned away and you have comforted me. Surely God is my salvation; I will trust and not be afraid. The Lord, the Lord, is my strength and my song; he has become my salvation.

A clear conscience

Our faith in Christ offers another peculiar comfort that no human sympathy can equal. For, in him, we can seek and obtain the forgiveness of God for our sins. So often, and so sadly, it seems that we are locked away in our own consciousness of guilt. For one thing we are not prepared to admit that we are wrong, but just go on pretending everything is all right. Yet confessing our sins to God can be the most liberating experience of life. Now we can trust and no longer be afraid – we were weak, but God has renewed our strength. We get up and go on in fellowship with him. This is comfort indeed.

Psalm 32:1–3, 5 Isaiah 12:1–2

The liberation of confession to God opens us to a comfort that is deep, and lasting.

Comfort that is clear

Comfort through confidence

The Lord is compassionate and gracious, slow to anger, abounding in love. He will not always accuse, nor will he harbour his anger for ever; he does not treat us as our sins deserve or repay us according to our iniquities. For as high as the heavens are above the earth, so great is his love for those who fear him; as far as the east is from the west, so far has he removed our transgressions from us. As a father has compassion on his children, so the Lord has compassion on those who fear him.

Therefore, there is now no condemnation for those who are in Christ Jesus, because through Christ Jesus the law of the Spirit of life set me free from the law of sin and death. For what the law was powerless to do in that it was weakened by the sinful nature, God did by sending his own Son in the likeness of sinful man to be a sin offering.

You can trust him!

Some of us need special assurance about forgiveness: our guiltiness seems to linger on, even though we are told that God will forgive. The Psalm shows us by how much God can forgive.

Paul, in the language of his legal training, insists that we must consider ourselves free and acquitted. For God has acted; he has met the demands of the law which might have condemned us. He has sent his own Son as an offering for sin – to put sin in the wrong and us in the right. There is no condemnation now!

Psalm 103:8–13 Romans 8:1–3

'As high as the heavens . . .
so great is God's love.'

Comfort that is surprising

Comfort in suffering

Consider it pure joy, my brothers, whenever you face trials of many kinds, because you know that the testing of your faith develops perseverance. Perseverance must finish its work so that you may be mature and complete, not lacking anything.

As servants of God we commend ourselves in every way . . . through glory and dishonour, bad report and good report; genuine, yet regarded as imposters; known, yet regarded as unknown; dying, and yet we live on; beaten, and yet not killed; sorrowful, yet always rejoicing; poor, yet making many rich; having nothing, and yet possessing everything.

Who shall separate us from the love of Christ? Shall trouble or hardship or persecution or famine or nakedness or danger or sword? As it is written: 'for your sake we face death all day long; we are considered as sheep to be slaughtered.' No, in all these things we are more than conquerors through him who loved us.

The fellowship of the cross

These Christian leaders have a new and positive outlook on suffering. Dedicate it, they say, to Christ. Then you will not only conquer it, but you will be able to help others through your suffering, just as Jesus did.

James 1:2–4   2 Corinthians 6:4, 8–10   Romans 8:35–37

Because Jesus suffered on the cross,
the Christian can face suffering with joy.

Comfort that is satisfying

Thank you, Lord!

Praise the Lord, O my soul; all my inmost being, praise his holy name. Praise the Lord, O my soul, and forget not all his benefits. He forgives all my sins and heals all my diseases; he redeems my life from the pit and crowns me with love and compassion. He satisfies my desires with good things, so that my youth is renewed like the eagle's.

I will exalt you, O Lord, for you lifted me out of the depths and did not let my enemies gloat over me. O Lord my God, I called to you for help and you healed me. O Lord, you brought me up from the grave; you spared me from going down into the pit. Sing to the Lord, you saints of his; praise his holy name. For his anger lasts only a moment, but his favour lasts a lifetime; weeping may remain for a night, but rejoicing comes in the morning.

How wonderful is God

It's only when we look back that we clearly see God's hand in our lives. Notice how these Psalms cover all sorts of conditions in which we might need to be comforted. Reading – or singing – the Psalms leaves you with a vivid impression of how wonderful God is. He is not daunted, like us, by temporary circumstances. That's why we need him so much. For we can feel different from one day to the next. God, our comforter, is eternal – praise his holy name.

Psalm 103:1–5 Psalm 30:1–5

'I will exalt you, O Lord, for you lifted me out of the depths.'

A prayer for comfort

O God
the Father of our Lord Jesus,
you gave your only Son
to die for our redemption
and to sorrow for our sin.
Look upon our pain and distress:
out of bitterness, bring the sweetness
of the knowledge of Christ,
and out of our present darkness,
the light of true faith in him,
now and for evermore. Amen.

Michael Perry

The Promise of
Confidence

The promise of confidence
Be assured – don't fret
Leave it to God

Confidence from certainty
Confidence based on fact
God is reliable

Confidence that acts
A calculated risk
God can use us

Confidence that bears fruit
Confidence and faith
You can hold your head high

Confidence in God's strength
God – the rock
Here we may be safe

Confidence in God's care
God – the shepherd
Here we shall find pasture

Confidence that cannot fail
Misplaced confidence – wealth
Who gives wealth?

Confidence beyond ourselves
Misplaced confidence – self-righteousness
Learn the lesson!

Confidence in God himself
Misplaced confidence in empty religion
Confidence beyond buildings

Confidence unshakable
Don't let others upset you
Wait and see!

A prayer for confidence

The promise of confidence

Be assured – don't fret

The Lord watches over you – the Lord is your shade at your right hand; the sun will not harm you by day, nor the moon by night. The Lord will keep you from all harm – he will watch over your life.

Jesus said: 'See how the lilies of the field grow. If that is how God clothes the grass of the field which is here today and tomorrow is thrown into the fire, will he not much more clothe you, O you of little faith? So do not worry, saying "What shall we eat?" or "What shall we drink?" or "What shall we wear?" for the pagans run after all these things, and your heavenly father knows that you need them.'

Leave it to God

It's all very well to say, 'Don't worry' when you haven't got responsibilities. But most of us have other people who depend on us. We cannot let them down, and so we worry about them even if we do not worry about ourselves. What we forget is that God, too, has his responsibilities! We are his responsibilities. and he is far less likely to fail us than we are to fail *our* dependents. He is our heavenly Father – faithful, reliable, and unchanging, he is watching over us all the time.

Jesus – in his Sermon on the Mount – says it's pagan to fuss and bother unduly about the peripheral things of life. He counsels us to concentrate upon the immediate problems in hand – the rest we can safely leave to God.

Psalm 121:5–7 Matthew 6:28, 30–32

Be confident in God's promises.

Confidence from certainty

Confidence based on fact

We know that in all things God works for the good of those who love him, who have been called according to his purpose. For those God foreknew he also predestined to be conformed to the likeness of his Son, that he might be the firstborn among many brothers. And those he predestined, he also called; those he called, he also justified; those he justified, he also glorified.

We know that we live in him and he in us, because he has given us of his Spirit. And we have seen and testify that the Father has sent his Son to be the Saviour of the world. If anyone acknowledges that Jesus is the Son of God, God lives in him and he in God. And so we know and rely on the love God has for us.

God is reliable

Our confidence is not based on superstition or guesswork. It is based on the reliability of God and his promises, and the experience of God's Holy Spirit in our lives.

The Bible warns us that outside Christ there can be little confidence and little certainty. God does not give a blanket assurance of his grace to all the world. Rather, he invites all sorts and conditions of people from every nation on earth to be his children. They become brothers and sisters in his mission and in his sufferings. If we suffer with him, says Paul, we shall also reign with him.

Romans 8:28–30 1 John 4:13–16

We rely on the love God has for us.

Confidence that acts

A calculated risk

David took his staff in his hand, chose five smooth stones from the stream, put them in the pouch of his shepherd's bag and, with his sling in his hand, approached the Philistine. David said to the Philistine, 'You come against me with sword and spear and javelin but I come against you in the name of the Lord Almighty, the God of the armies of Israel, whom you have defied. This day the Lord will hand you over to me. All those gathered here will know that it is not by sword or spear that the Lord saves; for the battle is the Lord's and he will give all of you into our hands.'

God can use us

Here is the famous story of a young lad who had every reason to be afraid. Had he let his mind dwell on his own weakness, he surely would have lost the fight. It was because he was prepared to do it in God's strength alone that he won. God could use, not the pretentious armour of the cowering generals, but the simple skills of the young shepherd. We need not fret because of status that we do not have. God is able and willing to use us as we are. This was David's great strength: his confidence in God and his intention to glorify not himself but his Lord. We too can be confident, if we have offered our lives in God's service. For we then have his authority and his Spirit's power.

1 Samuel 17:40–47 selection

This famous victory demonstrates confidence in God.

Confidence that bears fruit

Confidence and faith

The Lord says: '. . . Blessed is the man who trusts in the Lord, whose confidence is in him. He will be like a tree planted by the water that sends out its roots by the stream. It does not fear when heat comes.'

Whoever would love life and see good days must keep his tongue from evil and his lips from deceitful speech. He must turn from evil and do good; he must seek peace and pursue it. For the eyes of the Lord are on the righteous and his ears are attentive to their prayer, but the face of the Lord is against those who do evil.'

For the Lord God is a sun and shield; the Lord bestows favour and honour; no good thing does he withhold from those whose walk is blameless. O Lord Almighty, blessed is the man who trusts in you!

You can hold your head high

See the fruits of trusting God! a life of spiritual security. For trusting God means that we have resources not otherwise available. We can draw from God's strength to develop our lives. In times when 'the heat is on' we can shelter by his side. And we can have the confidence that we are not 'missing out' on anything; God will not hold anything back from us. Though we might value the honour of men and women, we should seek God's favour first. With confidence in him, we can hold our head up high. For those who trust God, there is a deep happiness in life – and a sense of worthy purpose.

Jeremiah 17:7, 8   1 Peter 3:10–12   Psalm 84:11, 12

'He will be like a tree planted by the waters.'

Confidence in God's strength

God – the rock

God is our refuge and strength, an ever present help in trouble. Therefore we will not fear though the earth give way and the mountains fall into the heart of the sea, though its waters roar and foam and the mountains quake with their surging. The Lord Almighty is with us, the God of Jacob is our fortress.

Hannah prayed and said: 'My heart rejoices in the Lord; in the Lord my horn is lifted high . . . There is no one holy like the Lord; there is no one besides you; there is no Rock like our God. Do not keep talking so proudly or let your mouth speak such arrogance, for the Lord is a God who knows, and by him deeds are weighed. The Lord brings death and makes alive; he brings down to the grave and raises up.'

Here we may be safe

In the midst of a changing world God is like a rock. He is our fortress. In him we take refuge when opposition is fierce. We are at risk if we put our confidence in anything else; no edifice of man will survive. But, though mountains shake and tremble, God cannot be moved by events. For he is finally in control of them. Therefore we should be still and recognise his supreme power. So shall our trust be in him alone.

Psalm 46:1–3, 7 1 Samuel 1:1–3

'The Lord is a strong tower to all who trust in him.'

Faith transfers us from doubt to certainty . . .

Confidence in God's care

God – the shepherd

The Lord is my shepherd, I shall lack nothing . . . he leads me beside quiet waters, he restores my soul. He guides me in paths of righteousness for his name's sake.

Jesus said: 'I am the Good Shepherd; I know my sheep and my sheep know me – just as the Father knows me and I know the Father – and I lay down my life for the sheep.

He will be their shepherd; he will lead them to springs of living water. And God will wipe away every tear from their eyes.

For you were like sheep going astray, but now you have returned to the Shepherd and Overseer of your souls.

Here we shall find pasture

This picture of God persists throughout the Bible, but it is quite different from the last. Here God's concern, compassion and attentiveness is shown. He loves us and finds us, wherever we get to in our wanderings. More positively than that, he chooses out our path for us. He refreshes and restores us. He shields us from eternal danger; for even in the valley of the shadow he is still there with us. All the more reason for us to return to him in whom is our confidence and our hope!

Psalm 23:1, 2, 3 John 10:14, 15 Revelation 7:17 1 Peter 2:25

'He refreshes and restores us'

Confidence that cannot fail

Misplaced confidence – wealth

Some trust in chariots and some in horses, but we trust in the name of the Lord our God. They are brought to their knees and fall, but we rise up and stand firm.

The Lord is with me; I will not be afraid. What can man do to me? The Lord is with me; he is my helper. I will look in triumph on my enemies. It is better to take refuge in the Lord than to trust in man. It is better to take refuge in the Lord than to trust in princes.

Command those who are rich in this present world not to be arrogant nor to put their hope in wealth, which is so uncertain, but to put their hope in God, who richly provides us with everything for our enjoyment. Command them to do good, to be rich in good deeds, and to be generous and willing to share. In this way they will lay up treasures for themselves as a firm foundation for the coming age, so that they may take hold of the life that is truly life.

Who gives wealth?

The temptations to trust in everything except God are all about us. Power, ambition and money are all-attractive. On the face of it, trusting in an invisible God cannot compete with them. We are so short-sighted, despite the lessons of history! Those who are rich or in power seem secure, but wealth evaporates. Money and goods are given to us by God for use in his service, not just for our own enjoyment and certainly not as a God-substitute.

Psalm 20:7, 8 Psalm 118:6–9 1 Timothy 6:17–19

A fairy-tale castle.
Wishful thinking gives us nothing.
The unseen God provides all things.

Confidence beyond ourselves

Misplaced confidence – self-righteousness

To some who were confident of their own righteousness and looked down on everybody else, Jesus told this parable. 'Two men went up to the temple to pray, one a Pharisee and the other a tax collector. The Pharisee stood up and prayed about himself: "God, I thank you that I am not like all other men – robbers, evil-doers, adulterers – or even like this tax collector. I fast twice a week and give a tenth of all I get." But the tax collector stood at a distance. He would not even look up to heaven, but beat his breast and said, "God, have mercy on me, a sinner." I tell you that this man, rather than the other, went home justified before God.'

Learn the lesson!

Jesus' classic story of the man who flaunted his achievements before God, warns us never to have confidence in anything that we might have done. Notice how this Pharisee prays about *himself*. The story shows that his faith is in himself and not in God. So many people like to think of themselves as Christians because they are quite good – or at least not all bad! This is not the Christianity that Jesus taught. For Jesus, it was the sinner in the story who was 'justified' – put right with God. God is not impressed by our claims of goodness – which will never meet his eternal standard. He is, however, responsive to our confessions of inadequacy. This may be the most important lesson we have to learn.

Luke 18:9–14

Acknowledging our weaknesses is the way to forgiveness.

Confidence in God himself

Misplaced confidence in empty religion

This is what the Lord Almighty, the God of Israel, says: 'Reform your ways, and your actions, and I will let you live in this place. Do not trust in deceptive words and say, "This is the temple of the Lord, the temple of the Lord, the temple of the Lord!" If you really change your ways and your actions and deal with each other justly . . . then I will let you live in this place, in the land I gave to your forefathers for ever and ever. But look, you are trusting in deceptive words that are worthless.'

Confidence beyond buildings

Another example of misplaced confidence! Jeremiah speaks to a people who claim to be religious but whose trust is more in their church building than their God. They have the temple – therefore they must be secure in the will of God. But they use the temple as many so-called religious people use their church building today – as a talisman.

Do we really think that by having a share in a church building we are secure in God's sight? – when, at the same time, our actions contradict the highest ideals of our faith, and our behaviour conflicts with God's commandments? So, is our confidence misplaced? Do we need reform and change, as Jeremiah suggests? Religious tradition is no substitute for godliness, and will not protect us from the judgement of God.

Jeremiah 7:3, 4, 7, 8

Man's structures collapse. Faith in God is permanent.

Confidence unshakable

Don't let others upset you

Trust in the Lord and do good; dwell in the land and enjoy safe pasture. Delight yourself in the Lord and he will give you the desires of your heart. Commit your way to the Lord; trust in him and he will do this: He will make your righteousness shine like the dawn, the justice of your cause like the noonday sun. Be still before the Lord and wait patiently for him; do not fret when men succeed in their ways, when they carry out their wicked schemes. Refrain from anger and turn from wrath; do not fret – it leads only to evil.

Jesus said: 'Seek first God's kingdom and his righteousness, and all these things will be given to you as well. Do not worry about tomorrow, for tomorrow will worry about itself. Each day has enough trouble of its own.'

Wait and see!

It is very easy to be diverted from a confident faith in God. There are other things that we naturally want more than pleasing him. Yet this is what God promises: If we take our delight in doing what he wants, he will make sure we don't lose out on life.

There are times when everyone but us seems to succeed – both honestly and dishonestly. God is testing our patience. We must wait for him. We can be sure that, in the end, we will be honoured for behaving in a godly way. The justice of our cause will be seen by all – without our contrivance. For the Lord is righteous, just, and all-powerful.

Psalm 37:3–8 Matthew 6:33, 34

'Delight yourself in the Lord' – every day.

A prayer for confidence

Lord Jesus,
I commit myself now
into your hands:
give me grace to see you,
to know your way,
to feel you near;
find me now in the quiet,
and hold me fast in the haste of the day,
for your name's sake.
Amen

Michael Perry